THE CLASSY
FORD V8

THE CLASSY FORD V8

BY LORIN SORENSEN

A Book About Those Terrific 1932-53 Fords and Mercurys in Tribute
to the 50th Anniversary of the Ford V8

A Silverado Publishing Company Book

OTHER BOOKS
BY LORIN SORENSEN

The American Ford
The Ford Shows
The Open Fords
The Ford Factory
The Ford Road

ACKNOWLEDGEMENTS

A special thanks to Mr. Doug Bakken, Director of the Ford Archives, Henry Ford Museum, Dearborn, Michigan, and to Dave Crippen, Archivist. Also to Wilfried Moellmann, Dick Gawne, and Bill Buffa of Ford Photomedia and to James C. Anderson and David Horvath of the Photographic Archives, University of Louisville, Louisville, Kentucky. And certainly thanks to Bob McCoppin, Jack Mulkey and Jim Connor.

PRODUCTION CREDITS

Lithography preparation, Dave Ruiz, Copy Production, Gail S. Mulkey, Assistant Photo Editor, John Sorensen, Production Assistant, Edy Sorensen, Copy Editor, Valerie Presten, Cover Illustration, Roy Jones, Graphic Services by Herdell Printing. Printed and bound by Kingsport Press, Kingsport, Tennessee.

Contents

ONE
Henry Ford's 1932 V8 Masterpiece 9

TWO
Those Dashing 1933-34 Model 40's 30

THREE
The Racy 1935-36 Fords 50

FOUR
Daring 1937-38 Streamlines 73

FIVE
The Stunning 1939-40 Models 96

SIX
Youthful 1941-42 Styling 120

SEVEN
Equipping the Ford V8 141

EIGHT
Young Henry's Post-war Cars 169

NINE
The All-American 1949-51 Models 185

TEN
Last of the Flathead Fords 219

Book trade distribution by

Motorbooks International
Publishers & Wholesalers Inc.
Osceola, Wisconsin 54020, USA

The Classy Ford V8 by Lorin Sorensen, Copyright 1982 by Silverado Publishing
Company, P.O. Box 393, St. Helena, California 94574. All rights reserved.
Library of Congress Catalog Number 82-80167. ISBN 0-942636-00-7

Foreword

On the 50th anniversary of the Ford V8 . . .

One of these days soon the V8-powered automobile will fade from the American scene and some folks will just shrug it off as another passing fancy. But it sure has given many of us a lot of pleasure over the years and the engine that blazed the trail will always be my favorite.

Henry Ford's flathead V8 car was more than a quick move and a pretty sound. It was the perfect harmony of beauty and performance under a rainbow of romance and adventure. Who from that era can forget those poetic body lines; or doesn't have a string of lively yarns to tell about old V8's they have known and loved? And who won't have an opinion about which of the 1932-53 Fords or Mercurys was the classiest?

As for me, I chose the car and the scene on the opposite page to sum up my idea of the *classy Ford V8.* The photo came into my hands by pure destiny and how it happened is one more V8 tale to be told.

Shortly before finishing this book I was invited south to speak before a group of Ford V8 enthusiasts. During dinner, my table had a lot of fun with movie trivia and when the subject of Gene Autry, Roy Rogers, Tim Holt, and some of our other matinee favorites came up, I said, "Well, they were all great but my idol was always Johnny Mack Brown." Only one fellow at the table ever remembered the star of "Ride 'Em Cowboy" and other flashbacks through a 12 year-old's mind. I left later, thinking that maybe Johnny Mack Brown wasn't so popular after all.

Three days later a newcomer to my town stopped by. It was Gary Perrin to tell me that he had found some early photos from his dad's dealership and that I was welcome to use any of them in this book. His father was Henry S. Perrin who ran a Ford agency by that name in Los Angeles during the thirties.

Shuffling through the small stack of old Perrin photos, what surfaces? Why none other than my hero Johnny Mack Brown with a pretty girl and one of the classiest Ford V8's you'll ever see!

So here's to you, Mr. Ford, for the wonderful V8. Your cars get prettier with age and the stories go on forever!

Lorin Sorensen

Lorin Sorensen, *author*

Film stars Johnny Mack Brown and Mona Barrie with one of the classiest Ford V8's ever— a 1934 Cabriolet.

Breezing along in a classy 1932 Deluxe Ford Roadster

Of all the autos dreamed up by Henry Ford none would have more lasting appeal and roadability than his swift V8's. The romance with the ''flatheads'' began in 1932 and has never waned.

ONE

Henry Ford's 1932 V8 Masterpiece

HARD times often bring out the best in a man's work, and Henry Ford's unveiling of the quick and classy Ford V8 during the lean days of the Great Depression would certainly rank high among his most brilliant achievements.

The ideas leading to the creation of this acclaimed automobile began to take root in the summer of 1931— probably around the auto maker's 68th birthday on the 30th of July. In those darkening days the nation's economy was in a tailspin; and on the very day before his birthday, Ford had been forced to lay off 75,000 assembly line workers idled by the lack of Model A business. Now the question that troubled him was not when the men would return, but whether they would resume building the 4-cylinder car at all.

Sales of the dandy little Model A had plummeted from a high of nearly two million cars in 1929 to less than half a million in the first six months of 1931, and there were certain signs that more than the economy was at fault. Sales figures didn't interest Henry Ford, but his keen eye had already detected that the Model A was losing its popularity. While it was the king of the low-priced fours, a good share of the market had been attracted to the competitive Chevrolets and Plymouths with their smooth new 6-cylinder engines.

Faced with reality and guided by the uncanny wisdom and insight that had not failed him in 28 years of tough decisions, the old master began to map a new plan in his mind.

A born tinkerer, he always had experiments of every conceivable kind underway in his shops, and for more than a decade had puttered unsuccessfully with a radical "X-8" engine concept. Unfortunately, this idea proved to be quite impractical because in chassis tests the powerplant's road-hugging bottom four spark plugs fouled easily in the dust and debris. At the same time, Ford Motor Company had a great deal of experience in building large V8 engines following its purchase of Lincoln Motor Company in 1922; and Henry Ford was duly impressed by the workings of the big car's Leland-designed V8.

While a pleasant thought, the idea of converting a Lincoln-type V8 to use in the smaller Ford cars was scotched by the high manufacturing cost. Where the Ford could be priced at rock bottom because the simple engine block was cast and machined in one piece, the fine Lincoln car sold at ten times the price partly because the intricate engine was cast and machined in separate units then carefully bench assembled.

But there could be a way to build a low priced V8 car that would leave those pesky Chevrolet "sixes" eating its dust!

Back in the summer of 1930 he had sent a trio of his most gifted experimental engineers to a small rustic building deep within the grounds of his public Greenfield Village showplace in Dearborn. This was a replica of Thomas Edison's Ft. Myers Laboratory and was authentic down to the old steam powered engine with its overhead shafts and belts that had helped the prolific inventor in his creative work.

One of the men sent to the Ft. Myers lab was the bright young German-born engineer Emil Zoerlein. Assigning him to the discreet location Henry Ford had said, "There are two more fellows working back there and what you see I want you to keep to yourself . . . We are designing a V8 engine, and I'd like you to work on the ignition and electrical equipment for it."

Reporting to the shop, Zoerlein found colleagues Carl Schultz and Ray Laird already at the drawing board laying out a small V8 engine that could, in theory, be mass produced. The two men were working from ideas suggested by Henry Ford and enhanced by them in rough paper sketches. "Schultz had made a layout of the V8 engine showing a box in front with about the same [distributor] position and shape as we

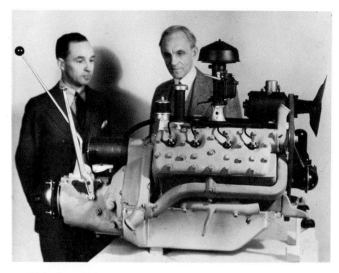

Edsel and Henry Ford with a prototype V8 engine

The V8 engine was nothing new when Henry Ford introduced it in his 1932 cars. In fact, the French Antoinette V8 was built in 1900 and Rolls Royce had one running in 1905. Ford's genius was to adapt it to mass production. Edsel loyally supported his father on the project and is credited with the graceful body styling. The two men are shown with an early 1932 V8 engine that has experimental starter location etc.

A production 1932 Ford V8 chassis at the Rouge plant

finally developed,'' recalled Zoerlein. "We designed a distributor with two pairs of breaker points . . . the same as the Model K Lincoln . . . except for a new housing. That wasn't very satisfactory to this application, but it was a start.''

To initiate the secret project Henry Ford had confided in no one, not even his own son Edsel who was Company president, nor Charles Sorensen, the tough production boss who was his closest aide. The veteran auto maker's born mechanical instincts were simply too delicate to be constantly challenged by the doubters. He had learned that lesson on the X8 project. If his new idea for a low cost V8 engine failed, then few would know of it. On the other hand, if it held promise he would have a neat trick to pull out of his hat at the proper time.

For nearly a year Henry Ford casually directed his trusted assistants on the quiet project. While Zoerlein experimented with the V8's electrical system, Schultz and Laird wrestled with the real puzzle . . . how to design a complex V8 engine block that could be cast in a single

piece? Finally, they were allowed to recruit Herman Reinholt, head of the Pattern Shop, and with his help secretly cast the first prototype block at the Rouge foundry. It seemed adequate and they were able to have it machined and fitted for running at the Ft. Myers workshop in early 1931.

Working with the scant equipment Mr. Ford provided them the men were now faced with a new problem . . . how to test the engine? Forbidden from driving so much as a nail into the Edison building they finally contrived a wooden stand that was wedged between the floor and ceiling. As Zoerlein recalled, ''We put a pulley on the back of the engine and ran it up to the steam engine powered transmission shaft of the shop to get it [the V8] started by belt drive . . . The engine started and the whole building shook. As it ran it would drive the line shaft and the steam engine to give it load until the belt slipped off. We were very happy because prior to starting the thing we didn't know whether it would run forward or backwards!''

While that first V8 engine did at times run

10

The V8 chassis was a superb engineering effort.

THE V8 ENGINE

Ford's famous flathead V8 engine for 1932 pioneered a successful series with its ingenious twin banks of four cylinders, each cast together with the crankcase and flywheel housing. This allowed a short, powerful crankshaft and installation of the 221 cubic inch 65hp engine in the same space required by a Four. Up front a single belt drove a pair of water pumps and generator-fan off the crank pulley. The 1932 belt was adjusted by turning a nut on the generator post mount. The aluminum intake manifold was topped by the generator, a Detroit Lubricator carburetor, and a fuel pump which ran by a push rod operating off the camshaft. Engine pans on the early models were cast aluminum and on later cars were stamped steel.

THE V8 CHASSIS

The 1932 Ford frame side members were unique in that they were shaped to form the exterior finish apron between the body and running boards. Actual wheelbase was 106-inches although Ford designated it 112-inches by measuring the distance from the center of the front spring to the center of the rear spring. Springs were transverse mounted and the front axle was stabilized with a radius rod ''wish bone,'' in the tradition of both the Model T and Model A. At the rear the gas tank neatly formed the underbody finish and the spare tire mount served also as a frame member. A system of rods and levers operated the four-wheel mechanical brakes, and wheels were 18-inch welded wire. The 1932 Ford V8 had a 3-speed transmission with synchronized second and high gears.

11

backwards and very rough, Henry Ford was pleased enough with the progress being made that in June, 1931, he invited Edsel and production bosses Sorensen and Martin out for a look. Also let in on the project was Lawrence Sheldrick who headed the Ford Engineering Department.

Edsel was easily convinced of the potential, but the other men flatly declared that a 90-degree V8 engine with crank throws at right angles simply could not be cast in one piece at mass production speeds, and that any attempt to do so would lead to catastrophe for the Company.

Ford's retort was, ''Anything that can be drawn up can be cast.''

Stung by the doubters, his ego battered, and losing millions on the Model A, Henry Ford ordered his foundrymen to start casting.

By the first of August he was working full bore on the project. On through the fall more men were thrown to the task of engineering, casting, and testing blocks. For every success there were a hundred failures from core shifts and pinholes, and still Henry Ford's determination held. Finally, on December 7, 1931, he made the momentous decision to stop all production of Model A passenger cars to concentrate on the development of a V8-powered replacement.

Thus began a $300 million gamble that the casting problems could be solved in time. ''It was an awful gamble,'' said one automobile man in retrospect. ''There is not a man in this business today who would— let alone could— make that bet.'' To test his audacity Henry Ford had set April 1, 1932— just 11 weeks away— as the scheduled delivery date for the new Ford V8.

''We were scared because of the rush,'' said a foundry worker. ''I worked night and day. We even forgot to go home, right through Christmas season. One day in the foundry we had exactly 100 per cent scrap. Everything was wrong. Not one engine came out right. Just think of this: there were 54 separate cores in that mold— 54 sand cores that had to stay put just exactly right for the valve sections and cylinders and everything in that engine block.''

Meanwhile, the entire Ford organization edged toward the brink of total disaster. Its trained labor force had been mostly laid off; the Company's cash flow had all but dried up; and desperate dealers either went broke or struggled along on the sales of parts and used cars.

''The cost was incredible,'' recalled one foundry production man. ''If it wasn't for Henry Ford's great personal wealth, the Company could have gone broke in casting that engine.''

Recognizing this, Charles Sorensen set aside his inner doubts about the engine and pitched in at the foundry. Armed with his knowledge of pattern making where he had begun at Ford 27 years before, the big Dane barked orders and drove his men relentlessly. In the end it was his personal touch that resolved the major problems and from those triumphant days forward he would carry the nickname ''Cast Iron Charlie.''

As the Rouge shops worked against the clock to build production V8 engines, Joe Galamb, the affable Polish-born designer who drew up the Model T and Model A body designs, worked under the articulate direction of Edsel Ford to fashion a full line of open and closed bodies for the new Ford V8. Taking their cue from the beautiful new Model K Lincoln that so embodied Edsel's artistic taste, the two men set as their objective a smaller adaptation that would incorporate the same sculptured lines and fine detailing.

Galamb's final drawings and mock-ups were coordinated at the same time with a chassis design being developed under Henry Ford's supervision by engineers Eugene Farkas and Emery Nador. Also heavily involved in this creative work were the outside body suppliers Briggs, Murray, and Budd who fine-tuned the approved stamping designs in anticipation of production orders.

With money and a lot of hard work, all the nuts and bolts of Henry Ford's dream would come together right on schedule. The first Ford V8 drove off the Rouge assembly line March 9, 1932. By the 29th every dealer in the United States had at least one car to show and on April 2nd, Americans got their first look at Henry's latest mechanical marvel.

Against a backdrop of national distress nearly six million people visited Ford showrooms to see the new V8 during the first two days of its introduction. The Company set up a permanent exhibit at its Woodward Avenue showroom at Highland Park, Michigan, and sponsored regional dealer shows around the country. At the Richmond assembly plant across the bay from San Francisco newsmen were taken up in a plane to photograph the word *Ford* spelled out with 1932 models while the public was invited to the San Francisco Civic Auditorium for a close look at the long awaited beauties.

The 1932 Ford line ready for viewing at the San Francisco Civic Auditorium

San Franciscans throng to see the revolutionary new Ford V8's April 2, 1932

The crowning touch was the "V8" emblem set off by a sculptured grille in French Gray.

For the first time performance was combined with beauty to give the Ford a youthful, sporting image. Here, San Francisco Mayor Rossi admires the new 1932 V8 at a preview. A newsman in attendance wrote, "In the new Ford cars the eye is caught by the bright beauty of the rustless steel headlamps and travels along the bead on the side of the hood toward the rear of the car— giving the impression of an arrow in flight. The bodies are fresh and modern from the gracefully rounded V-type radiator to the rear bumper. The convex lamps, full-crowned fenders and long, low running boards harmonize with the balance of design." Future 1932 fans would attest that it was the classic radiator shell of these models that gave the cars a lasting distinction.

Although interest in the Ford V8's ran high, most people had little money to buy them. For that reason Ford Motor Company went after available business by sponsoring a nation-wide series of "Open Air Salons" through its assembly branches. Held in the summer, these events treated visitors to free demonstration rides, movies about making Fords, and lectures on the V8 engine. At the left a night crowd evaluates the 1932 models at the Louisville plant. In the photo below a peewee golf course is the setting for a similar event in July, 1932, at Marysville, California. Among the eye-catching models on display is a Sport Coupe (left foreground) and a Deluxe 3-window Coupe (right foreground).

The public test drives the new Ford V8's at Louisville, Kentucky

An open air exhibit of the fetching 1932 Ford line at Marysville, California

There were some very good reasons for Ford to keep a 4-cylinder engine in the mix for 1932. For one thing there was the persistent problem with bad blocks, overheating, and oil consumption related to early V8 engine production. For another there was the wary buyer who could not be convinced that an "8" ran as cheaply or as reliably as a "4". To counter this, the Company sponsored a number of realiability events such as the one run in the Mojave Desert in mid-1932. Over a 32 mile course driver Eddie Pullen in a 1932 Ford V8 Victoria traveled 33,301 miles in 33 days and averaged 20mpg without incident. His run was co-sponsored by Pennzoil and he is shown below with a motorcycle escort and official timer. A glimpse of the 1932 Ford "Model B" engine may be seen at the right. Note the missing "V8" emblem on the headlamp bar. This, and plain hub caps with Ford script essentially distinguished Model B 4-cylinder cars from "Model 18" V8 cars.

Eddie Pullen points out that "V8" hub caps are different from "Model B"

Driver Eddie Pullen with his V8 Victoria at start of 1932 Ford-Pennzoil economy run

Servicing a 1932 Ford 4-cylinder ``Model B`` Standard Roadster

1932 Ford V8 closed car driving compartment

Inside features of the new Ford V8 were nearly as revolutionary as the outside ones. While the light switch remained at the horn button as on Model A, the key and ignition switch were ingeniously combined in an anti-theft unit at the steering column bracket. With the ignition toggle in the off position and the key removed the steering gear thus locked the front wheels for parking. The 80mph speedometer and engine controls were grouped in a handsome engine-turned oval trimmed with a stainless bead strip and mounted in a mahogany color instrument panel (walnut grain panel on later cars as above). Roadster-phaeton instrument panels did not have the separate finish belt rail but fit up under the roll of the cowl. Deluxe Coupe instrument panels had an open compartment to the right of the instrument cluster for parcel stowage. Sun visors on 1932 Fords hinged out of the way and the windshield opened out to the desired position with the aid of a pair of adjustable swing arms. Further ventilation was had by opening the cowl ventilator by means of the lever under the dash.

Classic 1932 Ford rear details

Stock Duolamp. A right hand unit was an accessory

7,241 (V8)
521 (4-cyl)

1932 Ford Victoria *body by Murray*

Edsel Ford gave his body designers free artistic rein in styling the 1932 Ford Victoria, and the result was a masterpiece of automobile coachwork. Sacrificing nothing in the way of seating capacity, the car combined beautifully sculptured detailing with a close-coupled, rear-bustled, body profile that gave it a rich European look. These were "special deluxe" in appointments and came fitted with cowl lamps, dome light, ash trays, arm rests, toggle grips and a choice of Broadcloth, Mohair, or Bedford Cord upholstery.

1,982 (V8)
739 (4-cyl)

1932 Ford Sport Coupe *body by Briggs*

Coupes came in three distinct body styles for 1932. Rarest of these was the Sport model with its strictly-for-looks stationary soft top and decorative landau bars. While projected as a Deluxe model, the car was actually delivered without cowl lamps. A unique feature was the rear curtain which opened with sliding seams to permit conversation with rumble seat passengers. The Standard (5-window) Coupes were also designed less the cowl lamps and represented traditional Ford coupe styling. Conveniences included an adjustable seat and a rear window that lowered. First Fords to ever have front-opening "suicide" doors were the classy Deluxe (3-window) Coupes. These were also the only 1932 models that could not be ordered with the optional fender mount spare tire and wheel because of the door swing. Besides the omission of the rear quarter window which gave them such sleek lines, these coupes were the only 1932 Ford models with a glove compartment in the instrument panel.

20,506 (V8)
  968 (4-cyl)

1932 Ford Deluxe Coupe *body by Murray*

28,904 (V8)
20,342 (4-cyl)

1932 Ford Standard Coupe *body by Murray*

Nearly three times as many Tudor Sedans as Fordors were sold in 1932, making them the most popular in the line. At the right two officials of the 1932 Indianapolis 500-mile race pose with a courtesy model loaned by Ford. Note the open cowl ventilator. On the Model A this was the location for the gas filler cap. The old gravity flow fuel system was supplanted on 1932 Fords with a mechanical pump bringing fuel from a rear tank.

Pioneering aspects of the 1932 Fords meant continuous changes. Early cars had a two-strap front license bracket while later ones had a single-strap mount. The early horn was motor driven, while the later (August) horn was vibrator type. Early (to November) cars had 20-louvre hoods, while later ones had 25 to improve cooling. Some of the changes were obvious while others, such as manufacturer source differences in contracted parts, were more subtle. Cars sold as Standard models were often made to appear Deluxe with the addition of accessory cowl lamps. Sedans for 1932 came in Tudor or Fordor styles with either Standard or Deluxe equipment. Deluxe models were equipped with dome and cowl lamps, toggle grips, and ash trays. The Deluxe Fordors also came with a robe rail.

18,880 (V8)   9,310 (Std V8)
2,620 (4-cyl)   4,116 (Std 4-cyl)

1932 Dlx Fordor Sedan *body by Briggs*

A fleet order of 25 new 1932 Ford Yellow Cabs is shown lined up on a bank of the Ohio River i

57,930 (V8)	18,836 (Dlx V8)	
36,553 (4-cyl)	4,077 (Dlx 4-cyl)	**1932 Ford Standard Tudor Sedan** *body by Briggs*

Louisville, Kentucky, September 25, 1932. All are Tudor Sedans and all but six are V8's.

923 (Dlx V8)   483 (Std V8)
281 (Dlx 4-cyl)   593 (Std 4-cyl)   **1932 Ford Deluxe Phaeton** *body by Briggs*

6,893 (Dlx V8)   520 (Std V8)
3,719 (Dlx 4-cyl)   948 (Std 4-cyl)   **1932 Ford Deluxe Roadster** *body by Briggs*

842 (V8)
41 (4-cyl)

1932 Ford Convertible Sedan *body by Murray*

5,499 (V8)
427 (4 cyl)

1932 Ford Cabriolet *body by Briggs*

All four types of open Fords for 1932 are shown here— two with roll-up side windows and two with side curtains— and all four were body styles carried over from the Model A. A novice should note the folding, removable windshield, rolled upper body, and side curtain snaps unique to the roadster-phaeton. Deluxe models came with windshield wings, and the Deluxe Roadster was equipped also with rumble seat and fender step pad. Twin top rests protected the rear deck when the Roadster top was in the relaxed position. The Cabriolet's smoothly tailored top fitted to roll-up windows gave the car the advantages of both an open and closed car. The rumble seat came standard as did an opening rear curtain that was fastened overhead. This would be the last year for the incomparable Ford Convertible Sedan with the striking side body configuration. Folding front seats gave passenger access to the back seat and the complex top easily raised or lowered by hand. Bedford Cord upholstery was an option on this car as well as the Cabriolet, and both cars had the chrome windshield frame like the Deluxe (3-window) Coupe. All four 1932 Ford soft-top models utilized a canvas boot to protect the top when it was laid back. Retail prices ranged from $410 for the Standard Roadster to $600 for the Convertible Sedan.

To complement the stylish 1932 passenger models, Ford designed a line of attractive commercial vehicles with a standard 4-cylinder engine and a V8 option for some types. Overall sheetmetal and trim was given a different treatment, but the light commercials had the car front bumper while trucks had a plain bar. The wood-bodied Station Wagon seated 8 on three seats. The body was built-up by Baker-Raulang of Cleveland and consisted of a maple frame with birch panels and basswood roof slats. Side window curtains stashed overhead on channels and the back window had a removable snap-on curtain.

14,259 (4-cyl)   1932 Ford Pickup *body by Briggs*

351 (V8)
1,032 (4-cyl)   1932 Ford Station Wagon *body by Baker-Raulang*

26

593 (4-cyl) 1932 Ford Open Cab Pickup *body by Briggs*

Sale of 1932 Open Cab commercial Fords dropped an astonishing 85 per cent from those attaincd by the 1931 Model A's. Less than 600 were sold worldwide to signal the nearing obsolescence of these types as buyers' attitudes were changing. The simple body with its non-collapsible, removeable top and side curtains, interchanged with the Pickup or Truck chassis but with little price break, Depression-wary buyers opted for the more practical closed cabs.

Rare 1932 Ford Open Cab

LeBaron Division of Briggs Manufacturing Company was given the Ford contract to convert a limited number of regular 1932 Tudor Sedans to Sedan Deliveries requested by fleet buyers such as Jewel Tea and Morton Salt. The modification amounted to closing off the side windows, installing a door in the rear panel, and laying a wood cargo deck. The interior was upholstered in artificial leather and paneled with Masonite. A production run took place in just the last few months of the 1932 model year which accounts for the rarity of these commercial sedans.

344 (4-cyl)
58 (V8)   1932 Ford Sedan Delivery *body by LeBaron*

27

Since the 1933 Fords did not make their appearance until mid-February, the 1932's stayed on the showroom floors until that time. The photos opposite were taken January 23, 1933, at a Louisville, Kentucky, store run by Ford Motor Company in the absence of a failed dealer.

Cash only on this 1932 Ford V8 Standard Coupe

Noting by a sign on his wall that "our terms are strictly cash," a Brady, Texas, dealer poses with two secretaries and a comely Coupe for a promotional photo. At the right, the counterpart to this car sits on a salesfloor flanked by a Standard Tudor Sedan, Pickup, and Convertible Sedan (extreme right). Display boards serve to acquaint customers with the finer points of the Ford V8's chassis refinements and the wide use of stainless steel throughout the car.

1932 Convertible Sedan (right) shares floor in a Ford-run agency

A smartly finished 1932 V8 Standard Coupe at the Ford store in Louisville, Kentucky

TWO

Those Dashing 1933-34 Model 40's

"CHANGING models every year is the curse of the industry," fumed Henry Ford as he inspected prototypes of the new models to succeed his magnificent, but already obsolete, 1932 cars.

It was mid-summer and despite the V8's strong debut a few months before, declining sales volume from plant shutdowns, Depression, and competition had changed Ford from one of the greatest U.S. money makers to one of the greatest U.S. money losers. People were saying openly that Ford Motor Company was washed up, that it was geared to a day that had passed, and that its 70 year-old owner might spend his accumulated hundreds of millions but that he would never be on top again. On the sales record the future didn't look good; Ford had fallen so far behind Chevrolet in the small car market that it had almost been caught by the oncoming Plymouth.

But the skeptics failed to consider the aging motor magnate's fierce tenacity. Determined to regain his lead, he approved sweeping changes in chassis and body design for the 1933 models and shrugged off the expense of adding smarter lines and more passenger comfort. Always the motor and chassis man, he bent to the task of improving the V8, while styling was left mainly to his quietly artistic son, Edsel.

Hampered by a strike in the Briggs body plant and slowed by production bottlenecks associated with building a longer, almost entirely new car from scratch, the old auto king finally got his latest creation before the public on February 9, 1933. Overall he was pleased as punch, and for general reference named the stylish cars his "Model 40's."

"The new Ford V8 with much roomier bodies, entirely new and decidedly attractive appearance is out," wrote an automobile columnist. "It's beauty is enhanced by the rakish angle of the radiator grille which coincides with those of the windshield, hood, and door lines. Fenders are of modern design, with wide skirts, and the construction eliminates the need for the old splash aprons below the radiator and above the running boards. Wire spoke wheels have been reduced to 17-inch in size and full length bumpers, front and rear, are styled with a painted horizontal stripe and a slight dip in the center."

Once again Henry Ford had orchestrated a brilliant automobile but it was introduced so late in the model year that, with little price advantage and scant promotion, the car had only a lukewarm public response. Further, the refusal to allow the 9,000 Ford dealers to use high-pressure sales tactics got the cars off to a slow start and allowed the high-flying Chevys to take

Classy lines of the new 1933 Model 40's launched a new era in Ford styling

In the dust of Model 18 came Henry Ford's racy new Model 40! A beaming young lady is ardent over this Fordor Sedan on the beach at San Francisco. Her car has the single painted horn, painted windshield frame and wiper, and is void of cowl lamps which makes it the Standard model. Destined to become legend for their impressive speed and lean, graceful lines, the new Model 40's came in eight basic body styles with a choice of V8 or 4-cylinder engines.

another commanding market lead.

Still, as the Model 40's took to the road, there were growing signs that a segment of the public felt that "Henry has a good car again." Delighted that his V8's were finally catching the buyer's fancy and feeling he could build no better car for the present, Ford decided to sit tight and let the market come to him. There would be little change to Model 40 for 1934.

However, in the realm of promotion there would be dramatic change!

The first fresh breeze of Ford publicity in years blew across Detroit in late October, 1933. Here, at Convention Hall, the Company set up a car and truck exhibit and invited more than two thousand suppliers (183 participated) to show products that went into the making of Fords.

The giant Ford Exposition of Progress was a spectacle that attracted thousands and set the stage for the veteran showman's return to the national ring.

While directing Model 40 refinements for the coming market, Henry Ford began swiftly laying plans to erect his own "Rotunda" show-place for a major Company exhibit at the 1934 World's Fair in Chicago. At the same time he stepped up his advertising and prepared to hold his first press preview of new models since introduction of the Model A.

On December 6, 1933, at the best-publicized auto event since the onset of the Depression, Henry and Edsel Ford hosted newsmen at Dearborn to preview the nicely up-dated 1934 versions of the Model 40. It was held a month

Dazzling 1934 Ford models at the Louisville plant. A trim 3-window Coupe stands in the foreground.

earlier than other automakers' press reviews and stole headlines as much for the glamorous new models as for the fact that this was the first occasion that Henry Ford had ever served an alcoholic beverage at a Company function. While beer and cigars were passed around, reporters were openly enthusiastic about the new V8's and sent out columns of praise.

"Changes in the appearance of the attractive car includes new hood, radiator and grille lines, a new instrument panel, and luxurious new upholstery treatment," wrote the reporter for *Automotive Industries*. "The curve in the grille has been eliminated and there is a new ornament surrounding the radiator cap. Hub caps and the spare tire-lock cover are also new, as is the V8 insignia on the grille. The fashionable bodies have the new 'clear vision' ventilating system similar to that in the new Lincoln cars.''

The 1934 models had just the right touches to make them a sensation, and to assure their place in the hearts of auto fans as perhaps the classiest Fords for all time.

Model 40 was Henry Ford's first two-year V8 series, and only subtle differences distinguish 1933 cars from 1934. As noted with the Coupe (facing page) and Cabriolet (below), the hub cap V8 insignias were different; 1933 hood louvres were curved (1934 were straight); 1933's had one hood handle (1934 had two); 1933 had deeper head lamp and cowl lamp buckets; 1933 had twin body pin stripes (1934 had triple); and the 1933 grille was lean and curved while the 1934 was deep, flat, and had wider reveal and fewer vertical bars. All 1933 Fords had black fenders regardless of body color, while the 1934's came in body color over all with black fenders an option.

A pretty Cabriolet awaits a buyer at a dealer's showroom, along with other 1933 Ford V8 models.

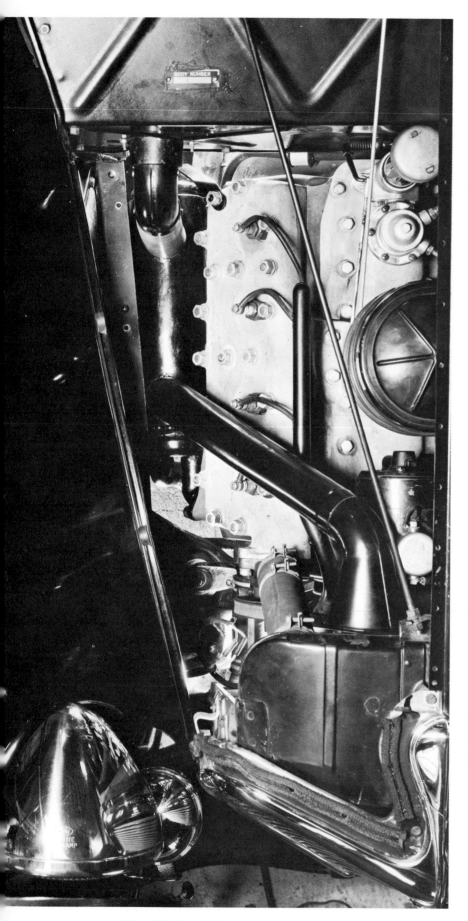

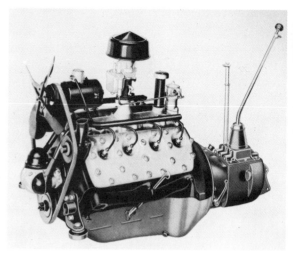

75hp 1933 Ford V8 engine

Aluminum cylinder heads, higher compression ratio, better cooling, and ignition added more horsepower to the Model 40 engines. The 1933 unit generated 75hp while the 1934 turned out 85hp. Power was gained in the 1934 engines by replacing the Detroit Lubricator carburetor with a dual downdraft Stromberg. In appearance the dressed engines differed by the shape of their air cleaners. An attachment was the fresh air heater (left) offered as an accessory in December, 1934, for the Model 40. The radiator fan blew warm air through the scoop, past an exhaust heater, and into the driving compartment.

85hp 1934 Ford V8 engine with fresh air heater duct

Ford engineered a swift chassis (1934 shown here) for the Model 40 cars.

A stiff X-type frame, combined with traditional transverse springing, and axles stabilized with radius rods gave the Model 40 chassis exceptional flexibility. This became a central theme in promoting the cars as seen at the Louisville, Kentucky, showroom to the left. The Deluxe Fordor Sedan is demonstrating how the Ford 3-point suspension allows the bodies to retain their fit regardless of chassis stress. The 3-window Coupe is set up in another example, while a Sedan has been laid over to expose highlighted chassis details.

1933 Fords give a showroom demonstration of superior Model 40 chassis traits

Removable side curtains took the place of roll-up side windows on the 1933-34 Ford Roadsters. Removable windshield assembly, fenders, and running boards also made these cars far and away the most successful of all the flathead V8's on the stock car tracks. An excellent power-to-weight ratio gave the cars a quickness that rewrote the records on dirt and gravel courses from Ascot to Elgin.

A flap in the roadster side-curtains allowed hand-signalling.

5,038 (V8)   4 (Std V8)
32 (4-cyl)

1934 Ford Deluxe Roadster *body by Murray*

EDSEL FORD'S 400 MI. PRIZE AND THE COMPETING DRIVERS

4,223 (V8)	126 (Std V8)
101 (4-cyl)	107 (Std 4-cyl)

1933 Ford Deluxe Roadster *body by Murray*

The 1933-34 Ford Roadsters were truly automobiles for sport. At the left a salesman at the Broadway showroom in New York City shows a demure prospect some of the features on a 1934 model. Roadsters in 1933-34 came Deluxe or Standard (just four Standards in 1934) which meant with or without cowl lamps, genuine leather seats, dual horns, or top boot. Windshield wings were optional both years.

Twelve of the 33 drivers slated to run in the 1933 "Indy 500" pose during a break in qualifications trials with a snazzy Ford Roadster donated by Edsel Ford for the leader at the end of 400 miles. At the extreme left is Tony Gulotta who finished 17th. Behind the headlight is Wilbur Shaw (28th) and the driver with the big grin to his left is Mauri Rose (2nd). Behind Rose is Fred Frame who won the 1932 classic but failed to qualify for this race. Looking serious and leaning on the car as though he owns it is "Wild Bill" Cummings (dark suit behind steering wheel). Cummings beat Rose by 27 seconds to win the race— and the Roadster.

7,852 (V8)
24 (4-cyl)

1933 Ford Cabriolet *body by Murray*

14,496 (V8)
12 (4-cyl)

1934 Ford Cabriolet *body by Murray*

The striking Model 40 Ford Cabriolets were richly upholstered in a choice of genuine leather or Bedford Cord.
Rumble seats were pleated in artificial leather and popped
open on a counterbalance by turning a handle behind the
driver's seat. While the early 1933 model pictured above
does not have the new right hand taillamp step pad, later
cars did and gave passengers getting into the rumble seat
proper footing to reach the other rubber step pad on the
fender.

3,128 (V8)   373 (Std V8)
412 (4-cyl)   377 (Std 4-cyl)

1934 Ford Deluxe Phaeton *body by Murray*

1,483 (V8)   232 (Std V8)
241 (4-cyl)   457 (Std 4-cyl)

1933 Ford Deluxe Phaeton *body by Murray*

Built for true road adventure, the Ford Phaetons for 1933-34 had the traditional canvas side curtains stowed in an envelope behind the rear seat back, ready for nasty weather, and a simple top that folded out of the way. Unlike 1932 models, the windshield did not fold, but the frame hinged out from the top for extra ventilation. Be-sides the usual detail differences in 1933-34 Fords, the 1933 Phaeton (and Roadster) had decidedly plainer door handles. A neat styling feature was the way the doors on the Model 40 Phaetons hinged from a concealed post which formed a truss with the driver's seat to stiffen the center of the body.

Richly finished in walnut burl-grain with deep mahogany tones, the 1933-34 Deluxe instrument panels were classic in design. Ford's technique for creating the real-wood effect began by transferring a picture of the desired grain to a composite roller. Stain was then applied to a blank sheet of steel, the grain-design rolled on, and the blank was finally dried, greased, and put in a press to be stamped out as the finished panel. The 1933-34 Standard instrument panels were painted Gray (early 1933), Maroon (late 1933), or Mahogany color (1934). Four types of panels were designed for passenger car use. These were the Deluxe or Standard varieties which differed by the ash tray and cigar lighter recess (Deluxe only); the Roadster-Phaeton type, which was narrower and fit up under the roll of the body cowl; and the Cabriolet-type as shown below which did not have the windshield ventilator knob opening. The significant difference between 1933-34 Ford panels is the engine-turned instrument insert as shown to the right.

1933 Fords featured engine-turned panel

A 1934 Ford Cabriolet with accessory glove compartment radio

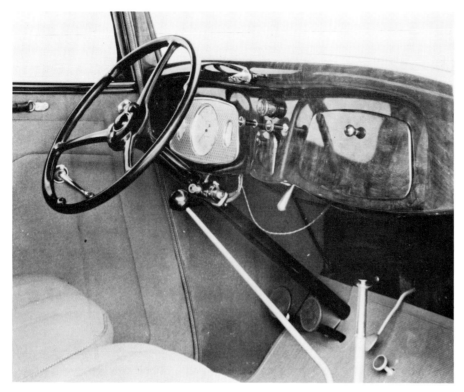

The 1934 Ford driving compartment was simply a refinement of the 1933 model. Door pulls especially evolved through the series varying from a hand stirrup (1933) to a pull strap (1933-34), a pull-to grip on the window moulding (early 1934 Standard), and finally to no pull at all. The door arm rest on the passenger side of 1934 Deluxe cars was eliminated at mid-year, and the 1934 Deluxe sun visors now swung to the side as well as down. All 1933's and the 1934 Standards had two-hinge type visors. Accessories available for both models included a glove compartment or ash tray radio, dual wipers, and heater—as pictured in the facing photos below.

Classic 1933 instrument panel was one of Ford's prettiest

Interior of a 1934 Ford Sedan equipped with ash tray radio and hot water heater

15,894 (V8)   6,585 (Std V8)
24 (4-cyl)   189 (Std 4-cyl)

1933 Ford Deluxe 3-Window Coupe *body by Murray*

Two types of Ford coupes were available in 1933-34. They were identified by the numbers of windows in the body, not counting the windshield. The less-expensive 5-window Coupes were more popular and a bit more practical, having room for a parcel shelf behind the seat. These coupes came in Standard or Deluxe and the rumble seat was available at extra cost. An excellent example of the spartan Standard 1933 model with the fabric tire cover (1933 Standard only) is the car in the lower photo on the opposite page.

1934 Ford Deluxe 5-Window Coupe *body by Murray*

26,879 (V8)   47,623 (Std V8)
3 (4-cyl)   20 (Std 4-cyl)

Designed specifically for the woman motorist, the 1933-34 Ford 3-window Coupes were very fashionable and found their greatest appeal among the sporting set. The rakish angle of the top, made possible by eliminating the side quarter windows, gave the cars the distinction which would add to their fame. Though a Standard version was offered in 1933, more than 90 per cent of this series was built with Deluxe features. As with the 5-window Coupes, these cars had a roll-down rear window that provided ventilation as well as a way to communicate with passengers in the optional rumble seat.

1934 Ford Deluxe 3-Window Coupe *body by Murray*

26,348 (V8)
7 (4-cyl)

31,797 (V8)   11,244 (Dlx V8)   1933 Ford Standard 5-Window Coupe *body by Briggs*
2,148 (4-cyl)   28 (Dlx 4-cyl)

4,193 (V8)
25 (4-cyl)

1933 Ford Victoria *body by Murray*

Elegantly styled, the 1933-34 Victorias were top-of-the-line in Ford cars. A refinement of the tudors, these models were especially distinguished by their sloping rear quarters and well-balanced design. Bodies on the 1933's were shorter and featured a slight bustle-back rear deck, and split front seats that folded like tudors'. The 1934 models had the slant-back deck, and seats that tilted up as a unit.

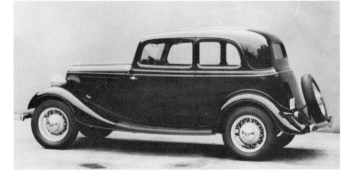

1933 Victorias did not have the rear deck opening

One of the most novel features of any Ford model in the thirties was the pull-back luggage compartment that was neatly concealed in the rear body of the 1934 Victorias. Close-coupled and rakishly handsome, these Victoria models were as classy as any sedans on the street. But when the driver wished to take extra baggage along on a trip, his car had a nice advantage. Releasing a lever behind the back seat cushion, the driver stepped to the rear and, as shown left, pulled back on the spare to draw out a compartment. Canvas bellows formed the sides and after the luggage was stowed, a spring-steel reinforced canvas coverlet was snapped on for snug all-weather protection. This feature was only available on the 1934 Ford Victoria and was never incorporated in a Ford design again. Longer taillight brackets, and more arch in the rear bumper were also unique to the 1934 Ford Victorias.

One-of-a-kind 1934 Victoria luggage compartment

20,083 (V8)   1934 Ford Victoria *body by Murray*

1933 Ford Deluxe Tudor Sedan *body by Briggs*

48,233 (V8)   106,387 (Std V8)
  85 (4-cyl)   2,911 (Std 4-cyl)

1934 Ford Standard Fordor Sedan *body by Briggs*

22,394 (V8)   102,268 (Dlx V8)
   405 (4-cyl)   384 (Dlx 4-cyl)

121,696 (V8)   124,870 (Std V8)
    12 (4-cyl)   185 (Std 4-cyl)
1934 Ford Deluxe Tudor Sedan *body by Briggs*

A new Ford V8 truck makes a dandy exhibit platform for an appealing 1934 Ford Tudor. Rotating drums on eccentrics hooked to a power take-off put the chassis in wobbly motion to demonstrate how smooth the body ride would be over the deepest ruts. At the upper left is a 1933 Tudor—just before leaving on a 10,000-mile Mobiloil economy run in which it averaged nearly 22 mpg.

45,443 (V8)	19,602 (Std V8)
179 (4-cyl)	682 (Std 4-cyl)

1933 Ford Deluxe Fordor Sedan *body by Murray*

For sale in the one-car showroom of a small rural dealer, a 1933 Deluxe Fordor Sedan offers a crisp three-quarter view. The most practical Fords for family use, these models still did not sell as well as the more stylish, better priced tudors. Both models were available in either Standard or Deluxe trim, with the 4-cylinder engine optional at $50 off the V8 car price.

Ford and the Briggs body contractor combined to produce a truly beautiful Sedan Delivery for the 1933-34 light parcel market. As with the Pickup and Station Wagon, a spare wheel and tire sunk into a welled fender on the right side came standard on these models. A metal drum cover was extra. The interior was smartly detailed with artificial leather split seats that permitted access to the cargo deck without stepping to the rear door.

Quite fashionable after their introduction in 1929, the Ford Station Wagons found popularity around country estates, golf courses, lodges, and depots. While Murray Corporation finished and assembled the 1933-34 body units, the maple, birch, and basswood was cut and milled at the Company's Iron Mountain plant in the upper Michigan woods. These rustic beauties were given front styling the same as the Standard passenger models. Notice that the 1933 example has the very early skirtless-type fenders.

All commercial type 1933-34 Fords with 112-inch wheelbase (units shown on these pages) came with the 4-cylinder engine. The optional V8 was $50 extra. The Pickups shared Truck styling, with a V8 grille badge and hubcap insignia distinguishing 8-cylinder units. The 1934's also had a "Ford V8" badge set in the hood louvres. Deleted at the end of the 1934 model year were the poorly selling Open Cab models— making the 1932-34 series one of the rarest Ford body types ever produced.

9,328
483 (4-cyl)   1934 Ford Sedan Delivery *body by LeBaron*

2,905
95 (4-cyl)   1934 Ford Station Wagon *body by Murray*

308
202 (4-cyl)
99 (1934 V8)
248 (1934 4-cyl)

1933 Ford Open Cab Pickup *body by Murray*

66,922
13,914 (4-cyl)   1934 Ford Pickup *body by Murray*

2,296
2,153 (4-cyl)   1933 Ford Sedan Delivery *body by LeBaron*

1933 Sedan Delivery rear door

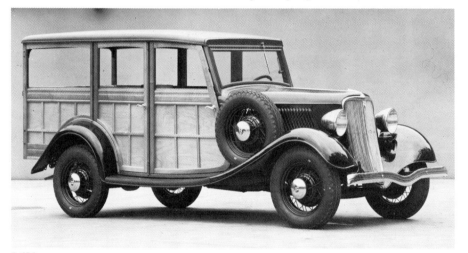

1,654
359 (4-cyl)   1933 Ford Station Wagon *body by Murray*

1933 Wagon with third seat out

33,748
14,815 (4-cyl)   1933 Ford Pickup *body by Murray*

THREE

The Racy 1935-36 Fords

HENRY Ford's dandy V8's had taken off like wildfire once people had a chance to get behind the wheel.   Among the car's earliest champions were lawmen who used its explosive speed to chase crooks— and crooks who stole them to outrun the law.   Dirt track and speed boat racers were quick to find that the sturdy flathead V8 would out perform anything its size and weight on land or water, and their sweep of the racing circuits from the Detroit River to Pikes Peak would become an American folk legend.

Even Henry Ford and his son Edsel got caught up in the racing fever and backed promoter Preston Tucker and famed engine-builder Harry Miller in developing some Ford V8 powered front-wheel-drive race cars for the 1935 Indianapolis 500 race.   They also signed on to loan the official pace car and a fleet of courtesy cars and trucks.   As it turned out, the engines ran fine but the radically designed racers went out with steering problems.

Meanwhile, the newly designed 1935 Fords were introduced to the public in late December, 1934, at the prestigious New York Auto Show. It had been 25 years since Ford had entered the annual event, and the Company captured much of the limelight with "motion" exhibits displayed at stands on three floors.   The displays drew attention to the new models and ranged from an operating "exploded" V8 engine and chassis, to a rapid engine assembly performed against the clock by two mechanics picked from Ford's big Rouge plant.

The theme for the 1935 models was "Greater Beauty, Greater Comfort, and Greater Safety."   As for design, the cars would have longer, wider bodies, more rounded curves, more windshield angle, and a narrower radiator grille treatment that gave the car a sleek wind-cutting appearance.   The proven 85hp engine had been modified for better crankcase ventilation and the car had better mechanical brakes, nicer steering, and a new "easy action" clutch.

Besides starring at New York and Indianapolis, the highlight of the 1935 Ford model year was the California-Pacific International Exposition at San Diego where the Company erected a special exhibit building.

But this was an era of fierce competition in the auto industry and while the cheers were heard over the unveiling of the 1935 cars, the Fords were at work planning even better 1936 models.

The second in a series being a refinement of the first, the 1936 Fords were indeed graceful and made their appearance in mid-October, 1935. Detailed to enhance its speedy reputation, the new model was bullet-shaped from its headlight lenses back.   The radiator grille, hood, and fenders were streamlined, and for the first time on a Ford the horns were behind grilles in the fender aprons and wheels were no longer wire spoke but a new drop-center type with a full disc hubcap.

The pace of razzle-dazzle promotion quickened in 1936 as Ford put on big shows at the Texas Centennial, Atlantic City Boardwalk, and at the Great Lakes Exposition in Cleveland. Not soon to be forgotten by those attending the shows were the parades featuring a Roadster on a float as "The Car in the Clouds."   Another crowd pleaser was the "Human Ford"— a 1936 Roadster that appeared on stage to ask and answer questions from the audience in a mystical "talking" voice.

The 1935-36 Fords were the third in the V8 body series. Parking lights were now inside the headlamps; the radiator cap had disappeared under the hood; bumpers now had two grooves; and horizontal bars accented the hood louvres. The 1935 models were the last Fords to have wire wheels and outside horns. The Convertible Sedan at the left, which paced the 1935 Indy "500," has extra show striping— as does the Roadster below shown with its manager and girls from the Lottie Mayer high-diving act at a theatre in Louisville, Kentucky.

Amelia Earhart in the dashing 1935 Indy "500" pace car

A 1936 Ford Roadster in show paint performs as the talking "Human Ford."

Absent from the Ford Line during 1933-34, the Convertible Sedan reappeared in 1935 featuring a conventional collapsible top. Roll-up window fit required a channel post, which was set between the raised door glass. When the top was down this important body extension was easily removed and stowed in a bag under the boot. Close cousins to the Ford touring sedans, these cars came with the moulding strip along the running boards. Two distinct varieties of the Ford convertible sedan were offered for 1936— the regular ''flat-back'' model, and the ''trunk-back'' type which replaced it in mid-year. The latter had a built-in luggage compartment with unique ''stubby'' taillights attached to the deck lid.

1936 Convertible Sedan (with trunk) body by Murray

4,234   1935 Ford Convertible Sedan *body by Murray*

5,601   1936 Ford Convertible Sedan *body by Murray*

Four pretty mermaids from the Lottie Mayer high-diving act promote a Louisville appearance by sporting around town in a 1936 Ford Convertible Sedan. This striking example is the so called "flat-back" model as compared to the car at the upper left. The girls were appearing at the National Theatre as part of a Ford promotion which featured a 1936 Ford Roadster as the mysterious talking "Human Ford."

105,157   1935 Ford Fordor Touring Sedan *body by Briggs*

159,825   1936 Ford Deluxe Fordor Touring Sedan *body by Briggs*

Parading the virtues of the 1935 Ford sedan ride

To meet public demand and the pressures of competition, Ford stylists designed a built-in trunk bulge on the rear stampings of the regular 1935-36 sedans. Fitted with a double-latched deck lid, this compartment readily separated the two distinct styles of closed sedans. A customer now had his choice of the smooth slant-back "sedan" or, for the large family that traveled a lot, the trunk-back "touring sedan" as shown on these pages. Available in Tudor or Fordor, the Touring Sedans only came in the Deluxe variety, and all were fitted with the stainless moulding trim along each running board.

At the upper left, four pretty passengers model the roominess and "Comfort Zone Riding Qualities" of a 1935 Ford Touring Sedan. The car rode on a float entered in a local parade by the Ford assembly plant in Louisville, Kentucky. It had been custom-finished inside and out, fitted with accessory chrome-spoke wheels, and stripped of doors and center-posts for the promotion.

87,326   1935 Ford Tudor Touring Sedan *body by Briggs*

125,303   1936 Ford Deluxe Tudor Touring Sedan *body by Briggs*

Except for the official body name, the 1935-36 bucket-seated Ford Tudor Sedans might have been another Victoria series. The company dropped that type after the 1934 model run, but these cars shared the same close-coupled styling, as expressed in the short roof line, large rear quarter window, and slanting deck. However, the elaborate tilt-out luggage compartment featured on the 1934 Victoria was not adapted to the new tudors. Instead, a small amount of storage space was available from inside by tilting the rear seatback forward. Besides the two passenger doors on each side, the fordor sedans also had three side windows.

In the photo below a traveling salesman for a liquor company in Louisville, Kentucky, poses with his puritan 1935 Standard Tudor Sedan before going on the road. At the lower right a dapper official at the 1935 Indianapolis "500" race is shown with a fordor loaned for the event by Ford Motor Company.

20,519
174,770 (Std) **1936 Ford Deluxe Tudor Sedan** *body by Briggs*

237,833
84,692 (Dlx) **1935 Ford Standard Tudor Sedan** *body by Briggs*

56

42,867
31,505 (Std)

1936 Ford Deluxe Fordor Sedan *body by Briggs*

ASST CHIEF STEWARD

OFFICIAL CAR

AAA

AAA REPRESENTATIVE

23RD INDIANAPOLIS 500 MILE RACE

75,807
49,176 (Std)

1935 Ford Deluxe Fordor Sedan *body by Briggs*

That the 1935-36 Ford 3-Window coupes shared the same basic body is obvious in these two photos. The arch-top doors were especially unique to this body style, and only the deluxe variety was produced. The rumble seat was an option, and we can observe that the fender step pad and upper deck handle on the 1935 model indicates this fair-weather accessory, while the car below does not have it. An envelope of tools and a jack were located in a special wooden box bolted on the right side of the rumble or luggage compartment.

31,513   1935 Ford 3-Window Coupe *body by Murray*

21,446   1936 Ford 3-Window Coupe *body by Murray*

Shorter roof line and absence of side quarter windows gave the Ford 3-Window Coupe wide appeal among the sporting set. The more conventional 5-window types were just right for the married couple or the traveling salesman. The 5-windows came in either Deluxe or Standard, as represented by the car at the top of the facing page which has the painted radiator grille and windshield frame.

78,477
33,065 (Dlx)

1935 Ford Standard 5-Window Coupe *body by Murray*

29,938
78,534 (Std)

1936 Ford Deluxe 5-Window Coupe *body by Murray*

A handsome couple and their 1935 Ford Deluxe 3-window Coupe

Going out for the evening a young lady powders her face, utilizing the accessory visor-vanity mirror, while her date lights up. This car also has an accessory radio mounted in the ash tray opening (center), with the receiver slung under the dash and the speaker between the sun visors. Ford stylists favored a painted finish on both Standard and Deluxe instrument panels for 1935 and for that reason wood-graining was not an option. An excellent view of the 3-window Coupe's unique door window shape, and the distinctive 1935 "double-bend" gear shift lever may be had from this angle.

Aside from the extensive use of wood-graining on later Deluxe panels (and the majority of Standard ones), 1936 Ford instrument panels were hardly different from the 1935's. Subtle dissimilarities were the control knobs' shape and color, instrument faces, and the design of the trim piece integral with the center ash tray. The 1936 model in the adjacent photo has the accessory steel-spoke "banjo" steering wheel first offered on a Ford February 28, 1936. As with other 1936 interior accessories, these came in Gray or Neutral Brown to match and were authorized for after-market installation on 1935 models as well.

Looking at the interior of a 1936 Ford Club Cabriolet through the back window

The cleanly-styled driving compartment of a 1936 Ford Deluxe Tudor Sedan

14,068

1936 Ford Cabriolet *body by Murray*

Workers at the Richmond, California, plant give a 1936 Ford Cabriolet final inspection at the end of the assembly line. Within the last 75 feet it had been given a floor mat, seat cushions, door adjustments, and the hood pin stripe was brushed on by hand. Traditionally the Ford Cabriolets had been all-weather close-cousins to the roadsters, with roll-up side windows and extra seating outside in the rumble seat. Then, in March, 1936, the Club Cabriolet was introduced featuring a top design enclosing a rear seat. At that, the less-expensive single-seat models finished out the year with 3-times the sales. From the side view the longer roof line distinguished the Club Cabriolet-type.

4,616   1936 Ford Club Cabriolet *body by Murray*

17,000   1935 Ford Cabriolet *body by Murray*

Assembling 1936 Ford 85hp V8 engines at the Richmond plant

Major elements in the delivery of a new Ford automobile are illustrated in these three scenes. All taken at the Richmond, California, assembly plant in March, 1936, the photos are striking in their clarity. Workers assemble fuel, cooling, and electrical systems to V8 engines in the scene above as the power plants, with transmissions attached, move toward the main line. In the view opposite that, Ford chassis units with the engines installed receive bodies assigned to them in the operation known as the "body drop." At the right, finished cars are driven outside to be delivered over to local dealers for driveaway, shipped out by truck haulaway, or loaded aboard outbound freight cars as shown here.

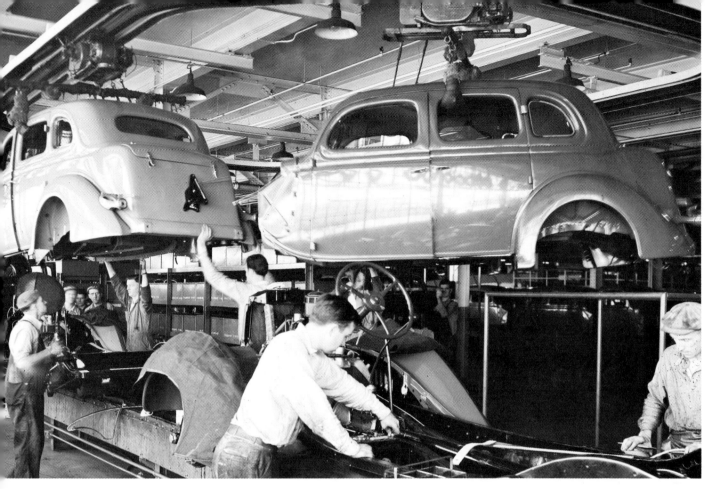

A pair of 1936 Fordor Touring Sedan bodies have been picked from storage to be mated with chassis.

Standard and Deluxe (door open) 1936 Fordor Sedans await loading in a boxcar for delivery to distant dealers.

Acres of new Ford cars and trucks crowd the delivery yard of the big Richmond, California, assembly plant in March, 1936. Beyond the rows of new units is the employees' parking area. A typical half-day's output, there are approximately 180 vehicles visible here. More than half of these are sedan types, with the rest a mix of coupes, cabriolets, pickups, trucks, and station wagons.

67

4,896   1935 Ford Roadster *body by Murray*

Following Ford tradition the sedan-type 1935-36 Phaetons and coupe-type Roadsters were best suited for fair weather climates— or the stout of heart. When skies threatened the driver was expected to pull over and remove side curtains from an envelope behind the rear seat cushion. These were installed on steel rods inserted in the special door grommets and were quickly shed when the sun reappeared. Owners of these classy V8's were much envied by America's youth who found the cars ideal for hot-rodding— especially the rumble-seated roadsters. At the lower right a Phaeton gets prime space at a 1935 Ford show in Chicago.

5,555   1936 Ford Phaeton *body by Murray*

3,862

1936 Ford Roadster *body by Murray*

6,073

1935 Ford Phaeton *body by Murray*

Quoting from the July 18, 1936, Ford press release; ''For prestige-building delivery equipment, the Ford V8 Sedan Delivery model is favored by many business men. The attractive hood and front design is the same as the passenger car, load space is 65-inches long, the floor is protected by steel skid strips, the interior is fully lined, and the wide rear door is hung on three hinges and is fitted with a friction device to hold it in the open position.'' Both the 1935 and 1936 models carried the spare in a side panel recess behind the optional passenger seat. An improvement made on 1936 units was an indented rear bumper to aid driver's reach into the cargo area.

8,308   1935 Ford Sedan Delivery *body by Briggs*

47,639   1935 Ford Pickup *body by Budd*   7,044   1936 Ford Statio

Dressed-up Ford Pickups at the right and above reflect the high regard businessmen of the period had for rolling promotion. Aware of this, Ford offered a Deluxe package on all Pickup and Truck units assembled after July 8, 1936. It included a ventilating split back window, dome lamp, dual wipers, sun visor, ash tray, cigar lighter, twin horns, and chrome windshield frame, rear view mirror, and radiator shell and grille. Obvious differences between 1935 and 1936 Ford Pickups are wheels, locations of the hood side emblem, and the radiator shell configuration. Greyhound cap and white body highlights on the Pickup above are add-ons. The Carl's Service units, of Louisville, Kentucky, are cleverly detailed in two-tones.

7,592
209 (Dlx)

1936 Ford Sedan Delivery *body by Briggs*

Ford expertise in developing sound hardwood bodies advanced buyers' interest further with release of the 1935-36 Station Wagon cabinetry. Beautifully panelled, varnished, and baked inside and out, the coachwork was further enhanced by new comforts such as the roll-up front door glass.

Wagon *body by Murray*

4,536

1935 Ford Station Wagon *body by Murray*

67,163
2,570 (Dlx)

1936 Ford Pickup *body by Budd*

Two engine types, tear-drop lines, all-steel bodies, and soft-action brakes made the 1937 Ford a sensation.

The owners of Cherokee Motors in Louisville, Kentucky, confidently await visitors to their showroom on introduction day of the new 1937 Ford models November 14, 1936. On the platform scattered with flower petals is a shiny Deluxe Fordor Sedan. The public reception to the racy body lines would have a lasting impact on the Company's futuristic styling efforts.

FOUR

Daring 1937-38 Streamlines

IT was the morning of November 6, 1936. The scene was the Detroit Coliseum where nearly 7,000 Ford dealers from all over the United States and Canada had gathered to preview the new 1937 models.

Finally the auditorium was darkened and a pencil of light picked out a V8 emblem on the center of the elevated stage. From the V8 emblem, golden-haired elves unwound themselves, and rising one at a time began tossing various car parts into a cauldron on the platform. Steam began to emerge as elements of engines, wheels, radiators and other assemblies were thrown into the brew. Then, in a fantasy of light and color, the fumes cleared, the elves disappeared, and a 1937 Ford Club Coupe rose up on a ramp, traversed the stage, and drove down to the Coliseum floor.

No dealer who saw the parade of beautiful new body types that followed the coupe down the aisle would come away with any doubt that 1937 was going to be a banner year.

Beautifully streamlined "tear drop" bodies, a choice of two V8 engines, cable-and-conduit brakes, improved "finger-tip" steering and other engineering innovations were the talk of the show. From a mechanical standpoint, the most sensational new feature was the small "economy" 60hp V8 engine offered as an option in Standard types and some commercial units. Although new to the North American continent, the little engine, which was two-thirds the size of the 85hp V8 and cost about four dollars less to produce, had been powering Ford cars in England and France for more than a year. It was hoped that the option would open a big market at home for a standard size car that was cheap to operate.

Within a week of the Detroit preview, the new 1937 Ford models were put on display in the dealerships as well as major exhibits arranged at the Hotel Astor, Park Lane Hotel, and the Company's metropolitan headquarters at 1710 Broadway in New York City. Later in the spring the cars would star in a special 90-day "Ford Miami Exposition."

In all, 1937 would live up to the great expectations. Aside from persistent complaints that Ford was out of step with the rest of the industry by not furnishing cars with hydraulic brakes, sales that season would not be topped for a dozen years.

The announcement of 1938 Ford models came at the end of November, 1937. With these cars the Ford sales and engineering staffs came up with a new approach to marketing. They simply reworked the front sheet metal on the 1937 coupe and sedan bodies and called them the "Standard" models, and made their fully restyled 1938 bodies the new "Deluxe" types.

This made the two passenger car lines totally different in appearance and broadened the sales appeal. Buyers now had the choice of the fashionable Deluxe models with the curved hood and grille shape and large tear-drop body, or the more sedate Standard cars with horizontal grille bars running backward along the side of the hood to form the louvres.

Perhaps it was the conservative styling of the 1938 line or the general dislike of the car's mechanical brakes versus hydraulics. Whatever the cause, buyers stayed away from the dealer showrooms in droves to make this the worst sales year for Ford since 1933.

But that did not seem to deter Henry Ford's strategy. He was already planning to bring out three distinct passenger types for the coming year.

1937 Ford dealer showroom

A giant-size customer gets the keys to a new 1937 Ford Standard Coupe

New 1937 Fords on display

Opposite: Two average-size Ford dealers, Mr. Check and Mr. Hutt, of Check-Hutt Motors in Louisville, Kentucky, deliver a new 1937 Ford Standard Coupe to a giant customer in late 1936. The big gent arrived for his car in the departing Ford Yellow Cab— a 15-cent ride to pick up his new purchase.

Billed by the company's ad agency as the most beautiful Fords yet, the 1937 models were a radical departure from past styling. Headlamps moulded into front fender aprons, highly crowned fenders, all-steel top and "shield-type" hood opening got high marks from dealers and customers alike. More colors, more options, more accessories, and the smaller V8-60 as a choice in some models added to the enthusiasm. Beyond the futuristic lines of this spring colored Deluxe Tudor Sedan sits a plain-but-pretty Standard Coupe and another Tudor. In the top photo on the opposite page, centered between two Deluxe Tudors, is a Deluxe Tudor Touring, distinguished by its trunk hump.

GRAND PRIZE
THIS
1937 *Ford* V8
4-DOOR SEDAN
WILL BE GIVEN AWAY
SUNDAY NIGHT
BILL WOOD MOTOR CO. LTD
AND FOOTHILL SPORTSMENS CLUB
TO THE PERSON HOLDING LUCKY NUMBER
See Complete line of New SPRING MODELS
NOW ON DISPLAY - BILLWOOD MOTOR CO.
Sales Floor 3001 E. 14 ST.

49,062
22,885 (Dlx)

1937 Ford Standard Fordor Sedan *body by Briggs*

Offered as the door prize at an Oakland, California, auto show, a comely 1937 Ford Sedan shines from the exhibit stand. Stacks of sales literature line the platform. The customer had eight kinds of Ford sedans to choose from in 1937. These were the ''slant-back'' models or the ''trunk-back'' touring sedans. Either could be had in Tudor or Fordor design with either the Standard or Deluxe features and a choice of the 85 or 60hp V8 engine. Standard models were readily identified by their painted radiator grilles and windshield frames. For the first time, all of the Ford sedan types provided access to the luggage compartment through a deck lid.

33,683
308,446 (Std)   1937 Ford Deluxe Tudor Sedan *body by Briggs*   73,690 (Dlx Touring)

98,687
45,531 (Std)   1937 Ford Deluxe Fordor Touring Sedan *body by Briggs*

"Slant-back" body design of 1937 tudor and fordor sedans featured luggage compartment deck lid.

1937 Ford Deluxe Fordor Sedan interior

The beautiful platinum-blonde traveler finds the roomy rear seat of a 1937 Ford Deluxe Sedan luxurious. Seats were wide, deep, and button-pillowed with broad pleats. Handy assist loops and arm rests added to the passenger's comfort. Window mouldings were metal with applied walnut woodgrain in Deluxe models and burl mahogany woodgrain in Standards. Upholstery options in the 1937 Ford sedans were mohair (shown here) or broadcloth, in taupe-colored shades.

The first Ford hard-top coupe with an enclosed rear seat made its debut with the introduction of 1937 models. Close-coupled and well-proportioned, the exciting new five-passenger Club Coupe was designed to carry extra riders in the rear quarter compartment by the nifty extension of the roof line and installation of a snug bench seat. Here, a gentleman offers the cozy recess to a pretty escort. Doors substantially wider than on the regular coupe, plus the split front seatback which tilted forward, allowed access to the back.

Stylish 1937 Ford Club Coupe was an all-new body type

16,992   1937 Ford Club Coupe *body by Murray*

80

1937 Dlx 5-W Coupe *body by Murray*

Above the belt-line the two varieties of Ford coupes for 1937 had distinctly different profiles. As for trim, the 5-window came in either Standard or Deluxe type, while the Club model was offered in Deluxe only. The single-seater had the traditional package tray and a seatback which tilted forward for optional access to the luggage compartment. A popular feature introduced on 1937 Fords was the "alligator-type" hood opening, as seen below— an innovation borrowed from the 1936 Lincoln-Zephyr and destined to set a lasting trend. Here, a Ford mechanic checks the engine compartment of a customer's brand new coupe with a portable unit which could monitor everything electrical on a Ford V8 from the distributor to the radio.

Troubleshooting the electrical system of a 1937 Ford Deluxe 5-Window Coupe

Opening-night in mid-July at Bacon-Pence

A time exposure captures the end of a warm evening at the new Bacon-Pence dealership in Louisville, Kentucky, July 9, 1938. The featured attraction was the cutaway V8 engine and chassis— being admired by the visitors in the lower right photo. The handsome front detail of the Deluxe Tudor Sedan in the window is seen at close hand below. This car has been dolled-up with white sidewall tires, full stainless wheel covers, center bumper guard, and road lamps, with prospects of attracting a well-heeled buyer.

A fully-equipped 1938 Ford Deluxe Tudor Sedan at Bacon-Pence

1938 Deluxe Fordor (left) and a Club Cabriolet on display at the Louisville assembly plant

Inside the Bacon-Pence showroom July 9, 1938

101,647   1938 Ford Deluxe Tudor Sedan *body by Briggs, Murray, or Budd*

106,117
30,287 (Std. Fordor)   1938 Ford Standard Tudor Sedan *body by Briggs, Murray, or Budd*

Louisville dealers get a stage preview of 1938 Ford models

Captivated Ford dealers watch the curtains roll back to unveil the new 1938 models at Memorial Auditorium in Louisville, Kentucky, November 10, 1937. On stage to the left is a Standard Fordor Sedan. In the middle on a turntable is a Deluxe Tudor, and on the right is a Standard Tudor. The Standard models had carry-over bodies from the 1937 Touring Sedans and are easily recognized by their front sheet-metal and rear deck bustle. On the facing page a quartet of Standard Tudors leave the Rouge plant aboard a 1937 Ford transport. Above that a Deluxe Tudor and Standard 5-window Coupe are shown on exhibit at the Detroit Auto Show.

92,020   1938 Ford Dlx Fordor *body by Briggs, Murray, or Budd*

Looking beyond a 1938 Ford Club Coupe at the crowd viewing cars at an assembly plant Open House

1938 Ford Deluxe Club Coupe *body by Murray*

34,059   1938 Ford Standard 5-Window Coupe *body by Murray*

22,225   1938 Ford Deluxe 5-Window Coupe *body by Murray*

The best known of the 1938 Ford Coupes was the Deluxe 5-window model— and yet more of the Standard variety were sold. A pretty lass poses in the car above which was on exhibit at the Detroit Auto Show. At the left dealers and their families compare a 1938 Standard model with a spiffy Deluxe Club Coupe at a preview in Louisville, Kentucky. Also in that city on May 24, 1938, the Ford assembly plant invited the public to the annual Open House. At the upper left visitors try out the back seat of a Club Coupe while the crowd beyond looks over the rest of the 1938 Ford line.

6,080   1938 Ford Deluxe Convertible Club Coupe *body by Murray*

4,702   1938 Ford Deluxe Convertible Coupe *body by Murray*

8,001

1937 Ford Club Cabriolet *body by Murray*

Recorded sales of the 1937-38 Ford Cabriolets indicate that buyers of these soft tops were torn between which type to purchase— the two-seat Club model, or the single-seat car. Both had roll-down side windows and a top that folded back into a recessed compartment for stowage beneath a snap-on boot. Both had optional genuine leather or Bedford Cord upholstery, and both came with Deluxe trim and the 85hp V8 engine. The difference was the price— whether to spend the extra money for the back seat or not. Ford's dilemma over which style to promote continued. Only the single-seat Convertible was available in 1939, and only the two-seat model in 1940.

10,184

1937 Ford Cabriolet *body by Murray*

While the 1937 Ford dash was considerably restyled from that of the previous year, the first big change in the V8 instrument panel came in 1938 when the radio speaker grille was incorporated as the dominant feature. Another notable change was the redesigned control knobs, which were now elongated in shape and recessed into the panel. Both of the 1937-38 Deluxe panels were straight-grain American Walnut and the 1937-38 Standards were finished in burl-grain Mahogany. Deluxe models came with the "banjo" steering wheel and a glove compartment clock and lock. The pretty driver to the left is shown operating the windshield opening knob.

1938 Ford Deluxe driving compartment

1938 Ford Standard instrument panel

1937 Ford instrument panel with optional radio

The snug interior of a 1937 Ford Club Cabriolet, showing the richly grained instrument panel and mouldings

1,250

1937 Ford Roadster *body by Murray*

The 1937 model would be the last of the sporty Ford road-sters since the type was first introduced in 1903. This would also be the only Ford roadster to have a fixed wind-shield frame and posts integral with the body. A close look-alike to the single seat 1937 Cabriolet and yet re-quiring side-curtain window enclosures, the identity and character of this Roadster had become so vague that the style was dropped in favor of the increasingly popular Cabriolet and Club Cabriolet models with roll-up side windows.

3,723   1937 Ford Touring Phaeton *body by Murray*

1,169   1938 Ford Deluxe Phaeton *body by Murray*

Declining production figures as seen at the bottom left of the photos above reflect demand and help explain why the Phaeton body type was finally dropped from the Ford line at the end of the 1938 model year. American habits had changed and motorists were more interested in cars for comfortable long-range driving. Besides, the Convertible Sedans now served this purpose and only differed by their higher price, roll-up windows, and more elaborate top mechanism and interior. The redundant styling actually makes it difficult to distinguish the 1937 or 1938 Phaetons from their Convertible Sedan counterparts when the tops are down. The giveaway, at a distance, is the side curtain snaps along the upper doors on Phaetons. Both types had removable side window equipment— curtains on the Phaetons, and center posts on the Convertible Sedans.

2,743   1938 Ford Deluxe Convertible Sedan *body by Murray*

4,378   1937 Ford Convertible Sedan *body by Murray*

2,672

1938 Ford Sedan Delivery *body by Briggs*

77,264
2,620 (Dlx)

1937 Ford Pickup *body by Budd*

All of the 1937 Commercial Cars (including Pickups) were available with either the improved 85hp V8 engine . . . or the new down-sized 60hp V8. While the smaller engine was recommended strictly for light-duty operations, many of these found their way into heavy use and earned undeserved ridicule. Still, the small engine fit a specific market and was carried over again with the 85hp in 1938. The 1937 Ford Pickup had increased load space, a new hood side and radiator shell treatment, and a split windshield. The 1938 Pickup was entirely redesigned with the new Ford truck line and featured a dominant oval radiator grille.

22,396

1938 Ford Pickup *body by Budd*

94

1937 Ford Sedan Delivery *body by Briggs*

"So smart that it has an immediate appeal to exclusive shops, yet so low priced that it is within the reach of all," the 1937 Ford Sedan Delivery was offered in both the Standard and Deluxe price brackets. The same body shell was utilized for the 1938 model but it was only offered with the Standard features. On this Delivery the spare tire was hung outside on the rear door.

9,304   1937 Ford Station Wagon *body by Murray*

1937 Wagon rear details

Camp car and delivery wagon, passenger car and bus, the handy Ford Station Wagon had built a reputation as being many vehicles in one. Telephone and electric companies were even using them to carry work crews and line gangs. The 1937 model came with an assist spring on the tailgate and optional glass sliding side windows. The 1938 Wagons were introduced with extra colors, lockable side window glass, and the spare was stowed out of the way behind the driver's seat, instead of the traditional place on the tailgate.

6,944   1938 Ford Station Wagon *body by Iron Mountain*

FIVE

The Stunning 1939-40 Models

TWO Ford milestones took place in November, 1938— the public showing of the brand new Mercury line, and the debut of hydraulic brakes on all 1939 vehicles.

Given to dealers to compete against Pontiac and Dodge in the medium-price field, the Mercury was Edsel Ford's creation. While a new design from the wheels up, it could more accurately be described as a "super deluxe Ford" with scaled-up price and proportions. It had a longer wheelbase by 4-inches, a roomier interior, nicer ride, and it came in four pretty body types, but its biggest selling point was the promise of owning the most luxurious Ford V8 that money could buy.

The car was a big press event during its introduction with the rest of the Ford line. *Automotive Industries* reported, "All bodies are extra wide, seating three passengers comfortably in both front and rear seats. The belt and cowl lines are low, giving good driver and passenger vision. Running boards are narrow and doors are wide for ease of entry. Special emphasis is laid on the quietness of the interiors, and it is claimed that with the windows closed it is possible for the passengers to converse without raising their voices— even at 70mph!"

Overshadowed by all the Mercury excitement were the other Ford V8s for 1939. Slightly outclassed but nonetheless stunning was the Deluxe model with its deep hood unbroken by louvres, low grille, wide-spaced headlights, and smooth body lines. The Standard version had elements of the 1938 Deluxe design with a full grille and short hood side louvres. It came with either the 85 or 60 hp V8 engine while the Deluxe model was powered by the 85hp engine only.

General interest in the 1939 Ford cars was furthered throughout the year by the Company's presence at the New York World's Fair. Here, as at Chicago, San Diego, and Dallas over the previous several years, a special building was erected to show the Ford drama. Visitors found a climax in "The Road of Tomorrow," an elevated highway encircling the entire main building, over which everyone had a chance to ride in Fords, Mercurys, or Lincoln Zephyrs.

In October the superb 1940 Ford models appeared in showrooms to a warm reception. Remembers auto dealer Merrill Jordan, "the workmanship on the convertible and station wagon was as good as that on any production automobile ever made." This is an especially notable comment in light of the fact that for the first time Ford had to build its own bodies.

Sealed-beam headlights and "finger-tip" shift lever mounted on the steering column were highlights of the 1940 models. And once again there were selections in Mercury, Ford Deluxe, and Ford Standard V8 body types. From a distance the new Mercurys looked just like the previous models but a closer look revealed differences in the grille, hood, hubcap, taillight treatment, and other components. The Ford Deluxe models featured a well-balanced front-end design set off by a cast center grille in chrome plate nestled between painted side grilles. This would be the last year for the Ford Standards and their special body sheet metal. However, rather than being a reworked 1939 Deluxe model, the 1940 Ford Standard had front design elements borrowed mainly from that year's pickup.

In April Ford built its 28-millionth car, a Deluxe Fordor Sedan assembled at the Edgewater, New Jersey, plant. Over the next several months it would travel throughout the U.S. stopping along the way in prominent cities and state capitals to collect license plates, and official autographs in the driver's log. Dealers lucky enough to have the car stop for the night invited their customers for a special showroom display featuring the milestone car and Ford motion pictures that helped boost interest throughout the 1940 line.

Unveiling of the new Mercury was a big event in the auto industry. In the photo opposite, a Sedan takes center stage between Standard and Deluxe 1939 Ford models at a dealer preview in Louisville, Kentucky.

A 1939 Ford Standard, a Deluxe Tudor, and a Mercury Town Sedan at Premier Motors

A 1939 Ford Deluxe Fordor ready for delivery outside Premier Motors in Louisville, Kentucky

Ford dealers were jubilant with introductions of the 1939 models because of all the consumer excitement over the new Mercury. In the photo to the left, the staff of Summers-Hermann in Louisville, Kentucky, holds for a showroom pose November 4, 1938,—just before the doors were opened to an evening crowd. In the foreground is a Deluxe Fordor and a dark Mercury Sedan. As seen in the line-up of cars on exhibit at the top of the opposite page, the dealer now had three distinct types to sell, the Standard model at the bottom of the line, the Deluxe for the average buyer, and the larger and more luxurious Mercury for the affluent. All this plus pleasing lines and hydraulic brakes added to a good year for Ford!

It's Ford for 1940! This classy coupe says it all.

Set out to attract prospects, a stunning Deluxe Business Coupe enhances the store front of Premier Motors in Louisville, Kentucky, October 7, 1939. The Deluxe Coupe represented some of the finer qualities of the Ford line for 1940— its sweeping lines showing all the grace and symmetry attainable in a two-passenger car of the era. At the right, a regular Convertible Coupe has been positioned on the salesfloor between a dressed-up Deluxe Tudor and the accessory department to stimulate interest in such trappings. Surely, no sport would want to take delivery of his new soft top without the dealer addition of a few genuine Ford items like the "single automatic tuning radio," or perhaps fender skirts, wheel covers, spot light, and sporty bumper tips.

A 1940 Ford Deluxe Tudor, a Convertible Coupe, and a Standard Fordor at Louisville Motors

"Opera" seats were a popular feature in 1940 Ford Standard and Deluxe Business Coupes

Having discontinued the Ford club coupe at the end of 1938, Ford stylists came back in 1940 with a neat idea that found a new market. They simply reworked the regular 5-window Coupe package compartment with space for a pair of jump seats and gave the area access by installing a split-back front seat. Nicknamed "Opera Coupe" by the public, but officially called the Business Coupe, the car in this configuration was ideal for the businessman or family with small children (or small adults). The fold-up jump seats hinged down from the side wall to stand on a peg while a padded rail served as a back rest.

Four types of Ford coupes were offered in 1940. The customer first had the option to purchase a Standard or Deluxe model, and then whether to get the Business Coupe with jump seats, or the 5-window Coupe with a single seat and package shelf. The Standard model shown on the facing page is a pleasant study in contrasts. Note the entirely different front-end, painted grille, headlamp doors, and distinct hubcaps. While one body shell served all four types, each Coupe design had its own special use and character.

33,693
16,785 (Bus. Coupe)

1940 Ford Standard 5-Window Coupe *body by Ford*

20,183
27,919 (5-W Coupe)

1940 Ford Deluxe Business Coupe *body by Ford*

Standard and Deluxe Ford Coupes for 1939 were two different cars from the windshield forward but shared the same dimensions inside. Both had luggage compartment access through the rear deck lid or by lifting the single seat back cushion, and both had large parcel shelves as well. In the photo below a smartly dressed Deluxe Coupe is classy transportation for a traveling salesman.

38,197 1939 Ford Std. 5-Window Coupe *body by Murray, Ford*

33,326   1939 Ford Deluxe 5-Window Coupe *body by Murray, Ford*

7,970   1939 Mercury Sedan Coupe *body by Murray, Ford*

Dropped from the Ford car line in 1938, the Club Coupe reappeared the following year with the introduction of the new Mercury. Designated the "Sedan Coupe," these two-seaters had more hip and leg room in the back compartment than the narrower, shorter wheelbase Fords. The 1940 Mercury Sedan Coupe was a sleek refinement of the '39 model and, in later years was widely customized by America's youth.

1940 Mercury Sedan Coupe from a pretty angle

15,107   1940 Mercury Sedan Coupe *body by Ford*

7,102   1939 Mercury Sport Convertible *body by Murray*

Sporty lines and a roomy rear seat gave the first Mercury Convertible a sales edge that helped boost sales of 1939 Ford cars to nearly double those in 1938. The 1940 Mercury Convertible was even more successful and proved to be one of the most popular V8's of all time. The top on the 1939 model lowered by hand, while that of the 1940 was lowered or raised at the pull of a knob under the dash which operated the new system powered by engine vacuum. Optional top fabric for both cars was colorful Tan-Gray with Tan edging, or Black with Vermilion edging.

9,212   1940 Mercury Sport Convertible *body by Lincoln*

Nothing could be finer than a warm sunny day, good
friends, and a 1940 Mercury Convertible. The automatic
top reclines on this beauty as two Michigan couples pre-
pare for an afternoon's adventure on the road.

10,422   1939 Ford Deluxe Convertible Coupe *body by Murray*

After five years of mediocre sales, the Convertible Sedan was finally dropped from the Ford line at the end of the 1939 production run. The all-weather body type reappeared the following year in the Mercury line-up but fared even worse as buyers shunned the expensive car as pretty but impractical. At the close of the 1940 model year the style was dropped completely. On the facing page a photographer covering a radio interview in front of a downtown Louisville, Kentucky, movie theatre, captures in his lens a rare Mercury Convertible Sedan parked at curb-side.

3,561   1939 Ford Deluxe Convertible Fordor Sedan *body by Murray*

The 1939 Convertible Coupe is notable for being the last Ford car to have a rumble seat. Sentimental as it was, the breezy rear deck arrangement had lost favor with buyers preferring the comforts of the enclosed club coupes first offered in 1936 (absent in 1939 but available in the new Mercury line.) The club coupe style was permanently adopted for all future convertible coupes beginning with the showy 1940 model which featured the new automatic top powered by engine vacuum.

23,704   1940 Ford Deluxe Convertible Club Coupe *body by Lincoln*

1,545   1940 Mercury Convertible Sedan *body by Lincoln*

Essentially the same stamping as the Deluxe, instrument panels on the 1940 Ford Standards were solid Briarwood Brown and had their own style instrument group. Control knobs, steering wheel, and other details had their own distinction also.

The 1940 Ford Standard dash differed from the Deluxe

A pretty driver models the fashionable front compartment of a 1940 Mercury Town Sedan

Breezing along in a sporty 1940 Ford Convertible Club Coupe

The 1940 Mercury instrument panel came in distinctive two-tones of blue plastic on silver steel and had the straight-line speedometer and gauges nicely grouped in front of the two-spoke steering wheel. Upholstery options were either blue-gray, bark-weave Broadcloth, or two-tone Bedford Cord in closed cars, and in saddle-brown or red-antique finish genuine leather in convertibles. Like the new Ford, the 1940 Mercury gear-shift lever was relocated from the floor to the column. A pistol-grip emergency brake handle and push-out ventilator handle are shown conveniently positioned under the dash.

An appealing color treatment in maroon and sand duotone distinguished the 1940 Ford Deluxe instrument panel and steering wheel from that of the Standard Ford or Mercury. An insert of styled plastic grouped the speedometer and gauges conveniently in front of the driver while a glove compartment clock and lock and ash trays at each extreme rounded out the ensemble. For installation of the accessory radio the decorative panel (under the girl's fingers) was removed to take the controls— with the chrome dash grille serving the speaker. The antenna was inserted through the cap in the dash and hole in the mirror bracket before exiting out the windshield header. Note the accessory hot water heater, and the delicate stitching pattern on the leather seat backs.

2,809   1939 Ford Sedan Delivery *body by Briggs*

Two distinct 1939 Ford styles to fascinate auto show visitors

Little changed from the 1938 model, the 1939 Ford Pickup would be the last to have a body built entirely by an outside supplier. Like some of the other 1939 Fords, it would also be the last to have the 60hp V8 option.

15,384   1939 Ford Pickup *body by Budd*

FORD

3,277   1939 Ford Standard Station Wagon *body by Iron Mountain*

Hydraulic brakes were the big news for the 1939 Fords and overshadowed any significant changes in the design of the commercials. However, two distinctive types of Stations Wagons were now available for the first time— either the Deluxe passenger type or the Standard type— in keeping with their new status as "passenger cars." As in 1938, the spare was again mounted inside both Wagons.

The 1939 Ford Sedan Delivery had the same Briggs body carried forward from 1935 and was styled the same as the Standard car. The photos above and to the lcft were taken at Detroit's Convention Hall November 13, 1938. Note the three different passenger car and truck front-end designs for 1939, and the wide range of body types.

6,155   1939 Ford Deluxe Station Wagon *body by Iron Mountain*

49,139

1940 Ford Pickup *body by Ford*

A two year-old Ford Pickup shows the wounds of the delivery trade in its job with a Louisville, Kentucky, distributor. In a dramatic shift away from the big truck look, the 1940 Pickups were given front-end treatment close to that of the Standard passenger models. The body belt line carried an intricate striping pattern and there was a choice of two-tone fender and body paint schemes.

4,886

1940 Ford Deluxe Sedan Delivery *body by Ford*

8,730   1940 Ford Deluxe Station Wagon *body by Iron Mountain*

4,469   1940 Ford Standard Station Wagon *body by Iron Mountain*

In keeping with the high calibre of styling associated with 1940 Ford models, a new body was designed for the Sedan Delivery. It came Deluxe only with the smart passenger car front-end and appointments. The fuel tank was mounted at mid-chassis with the filler projecting from the lower body side panel; and the spare tire was stowed underfloor inside the rear door. The classy Deliveries came equipped with a single driver's seat— a passenger unit being optional.

Smoothly shaped fabric-topped roof line, and better fitting joints with more refined maple contours gave the handsome 1940 Station Wagons peerless distinction. Both a Standard and a Deluxe type were offered, the generic difference being in metal styling and artificial leather throughout the Standard interior, versus genuine leather seat facings in the Deluxe. The spare tire returned to the tail gate mount on these models and was covered with a band and faceplate finished in body color.

115

Control knobs were set horizontally in the 1939 Ford instrument panel; the windshield-opener knob was moved to the top of the panel; and the radio speaker grille was restyled. The headlight switch was still at the horn button but the high beam was now controlled by a foot switch on the floor. Deluxe models came with the "banjo" steering wheel and a glove compartment clock and lock.

The 1939-40 Ford Tudor Sedans were available in four distinct front-end treatments, according to the buyer's desire of either Deluxe or Standard features. In the photo to the right, racy accessory fender skirts invite a police officer to chat with the young driver of a 1940 Deluxe Tudor about controlling his speed. Below that is a pose taken in San Francisco for a Ford ad. In the scene at the bottom of this page is a 1939 Deluxe Tudor at a Louisville, Kentucky, football game shortly before taking part in a half-time parade.

1939 Ford Deluxe Tudor interior

1939 Ford Standard dash   124,866   1939 Ford Standard Tudor Sedan *body by Ford*

144,333

1939 Ford Deluxe Tudor Sedan *body by Ford*

116

171,368   1940 Ford Deluxe Tudor Sedan *body by Ford*

150,933   1940 Ford Standard Tudor Sedan *body by Ford*

1939 Mercury Town Sedan *body by Briggs*
27,614
12,274 (Sedan)

1940 Mercury Town Sedan *body by Ford*
37,178
15,506 (Sedan)

A 1940 Ford Sedan wrapped for Christmas at the assembly plant

The abundance of Ford and Mercury sedan-types in 1939 and 1940 left the serious buyer little reason to wander off to look at the competition. Interestingly, the Ford Tudors were about three times as popular as the Fordors, while in the Mercury line it was the other way around. In the upper right photo Christmas season visitors to the Louisville assembly plant are enticed with a cellophane-wrapped Ford Deluxe Tudor. Beyond sits a shapely Deluxe Coupe. The angle of the Mercury to the right presents a good look at the "beer can" taillight well-remembered on this model.

On the facing page Ford's roving ambassador, Jimmy Rooney, waves from the Company's milestone 28-millionth car in front of a state capital. Rooney was the official greeter at the Rotunda in Dearborn and drove the car on a nationwide tour.

Plant showroom view beyond a swanky Mercury Town Sedan

118

91,756
25,545 (Std)

1940 Ford Deluxe Fordor Sedan *body by Ford*

SIX

Youthful 1941-42 Styling

MANY Americans were in a happy-go-lucky mood in 1941. There was a war raging overseas but Roosevelt's New Deal had put people back to work and gave them hope for renewed prosperity. At Ford Motor Company a man painting bodies was making good wages at $1.10 an hour, and a dingman repairing fender stampings had the best paying job on the assembly line at a few cents an hour more.

The past September, the new 1941 Ford and Mercurys were shown off to the press at a big reception in Dearborn. This would be the last time Henry Ford, now 78, would attend such an event and somehow sensing this, nearly 500 newsmen were on hand to hear his comments. True to form, the elderly automaker had little to say— letting the striking beauty and performance of his cars speak for themselves. Instead, he escorted the press party to a nearby site where the Company was erecting a huge plant to build fighter plane engines.

Ford was by now deeply committed to helping the government build American defense, and its solid record in past aviation work had the Company once again in the airplane business. The designs of the 1941 models reflected this fixation with aircraft as expressed in the twin air scoop styling of the three-piece Ford radiator grille.

"Probably the outstanding advancement in this year's cars is improved riding, made possible by a number of factors including a wheelbase increased to 114 inches," wrote Ford's own publication *Ford News*. "That the 1941 Ford V8 is a big car is indicated by the fact that the front seat in the Fordor Sedan is . . . a full seven inches wider than in any previous Ford car. The front-seat width . . . is why so little running board shows outside. The unusually wide bodies, with doors that round out at the bottom to cover all but a narrow strip of the running boards are trim and sleek. Headlamps are mounted far apart on the massive front fenders to increase nighttime visability and the separate parking lights are set high on the fenders."

Automotive writers would give the new Mercurys high ratings for elegant styling and plush interiors together with the smoother ride made possible by increasing the wheelbase to 118 inches. Both Ford and Mercury lines had the V8 engine but the big engineering news for 1941 was the six-cylinder option available to Ford passenger car buyers, and a 4-cylinder option offered in the commercial line. The two engines were developed to fill the continuing demand for economy in the void left by the discontinued 60hp V8.

On April 29th, Ford built its 29-millionth vehicle since the Company was founded in 1903, and on September 12th introduced its new 1942 line.

Produced against a backdrop of stepped-up defense work and government regulation, the new models were remarkably well-designed. Running boards were now fully concealed, rectangular parking lights were relocated on the front fender catwalks, body and fender lines were lavishly highlighted with bright trim, and grilles were massive.

Three days before Pearl Harbor, Ford was ordered by the government to freeze all future designs and to cut back on excessive options and use of brightwork. These orders were made all the more sober by the national declaration of war and the assumed conversion of Ford plants to all-out military production.

This assumption became reality on February 10, 1942, when all civilian car production was ordered frozen for the duration of the war. Consequently, the 1942 Fords and Mercurys were built over a very short span of five months— making these cars the rarest Fords in terms of numbers since 1910.

Styled for the young-at-heart, the 1941-42 Fords and Mercurys combined aspects of aviation design with campus fashion. Here, a winsome 1941 Mercury Convertible makes a pretty backdrop for a young suitor teaching his truelove the ancient game of mumbletypeg.

A pair of Deluxe and Super Deluxe Tudor Sedans glamorize a dealer's showroom in early 1941. Fading running boards and ballooned body proportions of these new models were at first startling to the public, but the overall clean lines and ready-for-action stance soon won over the doubters. Readily accepted as the latest in high-fashion motoring, these cars would become the leading edge of even bolder designs on the Company's drawing boards.

Her Christmas dreams come true! . . . a brand-new 1941 Mercury

Finger-tip seat adjustment before taking the 1941 Ford Super Deluxe Tudor for a spin

Rosemont Beige combined with Gray Elm-grain finish set off the beautiful 1941 Mercury instrument panel. Any driver was bound to feel important behind the car's classy steering wheel, also in Rosemont Beige with Casino Blue spoke inserts. In the photo opposite, it is a happy moment when she gets the best Christmas present of all!

One of the few dealer complaints about the 1941 Fords was that their trouser cuffs got caught on the seat adjustment lever getting in and out. This young lady demonstrates how really convenient it was. The handsome interior tailoring of her Super Deluxe Ford is enhanced by the smoothly styled instrument panel in Kelobra-grain finish with neutral-tone plastic trim.

Radio listeners looked forward to the weekly episodes of "One Man's Family." The Barbours are shown in real life riding down Sunset Boulevard in a 1941 Mercury Convertible during the annual Hollywood Christmas parade. Two-piece front fenders identify their car as a late production model.

Radio celebrities ride through Hollywood in a 1941 open Mercury

Both 1941 Ford and Mercury Convertible bodies were built at the Lincoln plant in Detroit and shared the same shell. The tops came in optional black or olive-drab material and the mechanisms were powered by twin electric motors that worked whether the engine was running or not. While the cars were very close in profile, the Mercurys were 4 inches longer, rode smoother, and had finer appointments.

8,157   1941 Mercury Convertible *body by Lincoln*

At the right a ball player arrives at the Detroit Tigers spring training camp at Lakeland, Florida, in his new 1941 Ford Convertible. On the opposite page two girls pose with their convertible and a pilot attached to the air command at Selfridge Field near Detroit. The girl's car has the accessory stainless front fender mouldings offered on cars in January to stem dealer's complaints about lack of a finished look. Their Ford also has optional side view mirrors installed in place of the short cowl trim.

Baseball players look over a new Ford Convertible in March, 1941

30,240   1941 Ford Super Deluxe Convertible Club Coupe *body by Lincoln*

Along with the new styling for 1941 the Ford line had no less than five Coupe options to offer with introduction of the Sedan Coupe body type. These included a variety of single-seat, jump seat, and club seat arrangements in a choice of Super Deluxe, Deluxe, or Special car models. The Sedan Coupe had a longer, more abrupt rear roof line than the 5-window, with the drip moulding ending at an angle with the belt line rather than sweeping along the rear deck. Likewise, the 1941-42 Mercury 5-window Coupes had a more sweeping profile than the regular Sedan types.

Henry Ford's loan of Rouge plant property in Dearborn for a pre-War Navy training school became a ready-made backdrop for Company photographers. On the facing page some swabbies check out the new model Sedan Coupes— and their alluring passengers. In the photo below a couple prepares to take a spin in their single seat Mercury.

33,598
12,844 (w/jump seats)
9,823 (Special)
22,878 (Sup Dlx)

1941 Ford Deluxe 5-Window Coupe *body by Ford*

45,977
10,796 (jump seats)

1941 Ford Super Deluxe Sedan Coupe *body by Ford*

1942 Mercury Coupe

718
4,942 (Sdn Cpe)

1942 Mercury 5-Window Coupe *body by Ford*

128

17.259
1,841 (jump seats)

1941 Mercury Sedan Coupe *body by Ford*

3,177 (5-W)

13,543
5,419 (Dlx)
5,936 (Dlx 5-W)

1942 Ford Super Deluxe Sedan Coupe *body by Ford*

5,411 (Sup Dlx 5-W)
1,606 (Spec. 5-W)

Six kinds of Sedans awaited the 1941 buyer and the same held true for 1942. These were the traditional Tudors and Fordors in the three trim and price ranges. This excessive duplication would lead the Office of Price Administration to order the auto industry to help conserve critical materials by doing away with such extras as accessories and multiple paint and upholstery options. Three days before Pearl Harbor it ordered a halt to the tooling on the new 1943 models altogether. Consequently, the 1942 models went through a retrenchment of features leading up to the final civilian car production shutdown for the duration of the War on February 10, 1942. The setting below typifies the mood of the Ford photographers as the nation got on a war footing.

88,053
25,928 (Dlx)
3,838 (Spec)

1941 Ford Super Deluxe Fordor Sedan *body by Ford*

37,199
27,302 (Dlx)
3,187 (Spec)

1942 Ford Super Deluxe Tudor Sedan *body by Ford*

185,788
177,018 (Dlx)
27,189 (Spec)

1941 Ford Super Deluxe Tudor Sedan *body by Ford*

The rear body treatment of the 1942 Ford Sedan would be a strong clue as to the shape of the next peace-time series of Fords. Meanwhile, the Ford Motor Company would put all of its industry toward production of military equipment for the duration of World War II.

The austere 1942 Ford Special had limited brightwork to help the war effort.

24,846
5,127 (Dlx)
11,578 (Spec)

1942 Ford Super Deluxe Fordor Sedan *body by Ford*

1942 Mercury closed car interior

For comparison a pretty Ford secretary models the driving compartments of 1942 Ford and Mercury closed cars. Note the entirely different instrument trim. Roomier Mercury closed cars came in Bedford Cord or Broadcloth with mouldings and dash grained in Light Silver Walnut or Mahogany Sequoia.

1942 Ford Super Deluxe closed car interior

Attractive Ford dash came in three grains for 1942: Kelobra on the Specials; crackle Mahogany on the Deluxe; and
Sequoia in burl grain, as shown here. Trim and knobs
were durable plastic. Upholstery options were grades of
Mohair or Broadcloth.

On display at Laney Motor Sales in Beaver, Pennsylvania, during the summer of 1941 a new Mercury Sedan awaits a buyer. This car presents a conservative contrast to the bolder-styled 1942 models below. An option on 1941 Mercurys, but not on the 1942's, was a choice of two-tone paint schemes. A new option for the 1942 Mercury buyer was a semi-automatic "Liquamatic Drive" transmission.

18,983
38,848 (Twn Sdn)   1941 Mercury Sedan *body by Ford*

Out for a spin in their new Mercury, Michigan tourists stop at Ford's Nankin Mills engraving shop to see how the Ford "script" name was etched into, or imprinted on, every item produced by the Company. Their car is a 2-door "sedan" model versus the 4-door "town sedan" type shown below.

4,820   1942 Mercury Sedan *body by Ford*

Ford's work with aircraft projects in defense work heavily influenced the styling of 1942 models. Here, a Mercury matches "airstream" design with that of an airplane. The massive use of bright trim on these models was ill-timed in light of the government's late-1941 crackdown on the auto industry's extravagant use of strategic metals.

10,475   1942 Mercury Town Sedan *body by Ford*

134

Their numbers cut short by the abrupt halt of civilian car production at the onset of World War II, the 1942 Ford and Mercury convertibles are among the rarest Ford automobiles ever produced. In fact, no actual photos of the Ford model exist among the thousands on file in the Ford Archives. A Mercury counterpart is shown below on the stage at Ford's famous Rotunda showplace in Dearborn, during a preview of new models. Both convertibles could be ordered with a choice of Tan, Red, or Blue genuine leather upholstery. The Ford was priced at $1418 and the Mercury had a suggested retail price of $1595.

2,920   1942 Ford Super Dlx Convt. Coupe *body by Lincoln*

956   1942 Mercury Club Convertible *body by Lincoln*

5,483
567 (Dlx)

1942 Ford Super Deluxe Station Wagon *body by Iron Mountain*

The first Mercury Station Wagon joined the Ford Motor Company product line with the introduction of 1941 models. Now the customer had a choice of three price and style categories, including the top-of-the-Ford-line Super Deluxe and the plainer Deluxe job.

2,143   1941 Mercury Station Wagon *body by Iron Mountain*

About ninety per cent of the wood used in building the Ford Station Wagon bodies was hard Maple, with the remainder in Birch— but the two were never mixed. The natural panels were usually gum wood, a soft veneer taken mostly from the inner Birch tree, and sometimes from other trees native to the Upper Michigan woods. The Super Deluxe Fords and Mercurys, however, had imported Mahogany panelling.

9,485
6,116 (Dlx)

1941 Ford Super Deluxe Station Wagon *body by Iron Mountain*

783

1942 Mercury Station Wagon *body by Iron Mountain*

46,096

1941 Ford Pickup *body by Ford*

Outwardly, the 1941 Ford Pickup was little changed from the 1940 model except for a new hood prow treatment, hub caps, and hood side emblem. Engine options were the V8 or choice of a new 6-cylinder or the 4-cylinder tractor powerplant (the first Ford Six since 1908 and the first offer of a Four since 1934). Two-tone colors were also optional, as were dual taillights. The 1942 models were a radical departure in styling with a bold flat front and enameled mouldings. Parking lights were set outboard on the fenders.

4,846

1941 Ford Sedan Delivery *body by Ford*

17,996   1942 Ford Pickup *body by Ford*

1,274   1942 Ford Sedan Delivery *body by Ford*

An unusual hybrid of Standard and Deluxe 1940-41 front-end parts, plus a one-of-a-kind hood ornament put the 1941 Ford Sedan Delivery in a category with the light commercial styling rather than with the passenger car line. The 1942 models had an all-new body with concealed running boards and fuel filler lid and once again had the passenger car front treatment. The American Tobacco Company Delivery shown has the painted grille frame unique to post-Pearl Harbor 1942 Fords, owing to the shortage of chrome.

A 1933 Ford Victoria body with Rose Beige Mohair upholstery— one of two customer options

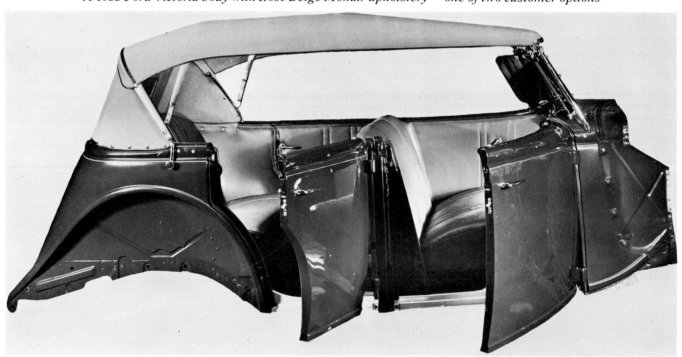

5,555

1936 Ford Phaeton *body by Murray* ⟵ *body supplier*

number produced

body type

Ford body types throughout the 1932-42 section of this book are captioned with U.S. or world production figures and the body maker as shown above. Bodies beyond 1940 were all made by Ford and Lincoln plants with some stampings by outside suppliers.

SEVEN

Equipping the Ford V8

JUST like today, the early Ford V8 buyer had two ways to select a car with the right style, color, and trappings that suited his particular taste and pocket book. He could pick one directly off the showroom floor or he could thumb through the sales catalogs, upholstery samples and paint chips and have the dealer order him one to his own liking.

In actual practice, the customer special order made up a very small part of the Ford business. Rather, cars were ordered for stock by the dealer based on what he thought would sell in his market. The accumulation of all these dealer orders plus calculated estimates from the Company sales office made up the assembly plant schedules as to what mix of body types and trim combinations to build. In other words, on a given day, the assembly line superintendent at Dallas might receive instructions to produce one special order Bambalina Blue Cabriolet with leather upholstery, and twenty others— 30 per cent of which should be Black with half genuine leather and the other half in bedford cord. As the cars went out to dealers and the results were tabulated, trends were quickly established and the sales headquarters was able to react by adjusting body types, colors, and trim selections— or to delete slow moving ones.

Thus the production of the Ford V8 was a colorful blend of body shapes, options, and accessories created as much by good business judgement as by anything else. Add to that the constant engineering and styling changes made to upgrade and sell the product, the variables of parts that might have each outside supplier's unique imprint, the choice of assembly technique at the particular plant, and the result was a single mass-produced Ford off the line like no other one behind it.

BODIES

The wide choice of open and closed body types offered on the V8 chassis in the early years was made possible by the talented styling departments of Ford and its competitive suppliers, while after 1940 the selections became more limited.

Except for a brief period at the end of Model T production, virtually all pre-1940 Ford bodies were supplied by outside makers. In the early V8 years these were Briggs Manufacturing Company, Murray Corporation of America, Edward G. Budd Manufacturing Company, LeBaron (a division of Briggs), and Baker-Raulang. In 1938, Ford's Iron Mountain plant began building complete station wagon bodies instead of furnishing the hardwood components for Murray to build up; and in 1940 the Company's Lincoln body plant began building Ford and Mercury convertibles. That same year Ford had completed its huge body plant at the Rouge and began producing its own car and truck body requirements.

OPTIONS

Within design schemes set by the Company, Ford V8's could be had in a pretty fair range of colors, upholstery fabrics, and Standard or Deluxe trimming. When offered, a rumble seat was an option at extra cost in open and closed coupes that did not already have that as standard equipment. The 1932-34 welled fenders with side mount spares were also options that could be installed to order at the assembly plants.

ACCESSORIES

The majority of Ford V8 accessories were sold and installed at the dealership because these were the source of extra profit and incentive. Some were easily attached while others, like dual windshield wipers, required a template and careful drilling and fitting. Accessories installed on the assembly line were generally ordered in combinations with a set value to help the dealer's purchase decision. It was at the dealership that the car was custom-fitted to the buyer and it was not uncommon to put leftover 1936 accessories on 1937 cars, etc. It was also common practice for the dealer to add requested paint details, body underseal, special wheels and tires, and other aftermarket accessories.

1932 FORD STANDARDS AND OPTIONS

Engine: *65hp V8 or 50hp 4-cyl*, Transmission: *3-speed manual*, Wheelbase: *112-inches*

CAR COLORS

BODY	MOULDING	★FENDERS	STRIPE	★★WHEELS
Black	*Black*	*Black*	*Gold*	*Apple Green*
Ford Med. Maroon	*Black*	*Black*	*Gold*	*Aurora Red*
Brewster Green Med.	*Brewster Green Lt.*	*Black*	*Silver Gray*	*Apple Green*
Tunis Gray	*Old Chester Gray*	*Black*	*Tacoma Cream*	*Tacoma Cream*
Old Chester Gray	*Tunis Gray*	*Black*	*Tacoma Cream*	*Tacoma Cream*
Washington Blue Med.	*Black*	*Black*	*Tacoma Cream*	*Tacoma Cream*
Brewster Green Lt.	☆☆*Brewster Green Med.*	*Black*	*Silver Gray*	*Apple Green*
Winterleaf Brown Lt.	*Winterleaf Brown Dk.*	*Black*	*Tacoma Cream*	*Tacoma Cream*
Emperor Brown Lt.	*Emperor Brown Dk*	*Black*	☆*Silver Gray*	*Tacoma Cream*

★ includes frame side rails, lamp brackets and sheet metal below body
★★*Black* wheels as standard on Standard cars. Wheels in colors optional on all cars at extra cost.
☆☆and upper body   ☆ or *Tacoma Cream*

INSTRUMENT PANEL

Early models *Mahogany color*, Later models *Mahogany stained Walnut grain*

UPHOLSTERY

	Copra Drab Genuine Leather	Artificial Leather	Russet Brown Genuine Leather	Mohair	Broadcloth	Bedford Cord	Wool Cloth
Standard Phaeton	—	yes	—	—	—	—	—
Deluxe Phaeton	yes	—	—	—	—	—	—
Standard Roadster	—	yes	—	—	—	—	—
Deluxe Roadster	yes	—	—	—	—	—	—
Standard Coupe	—	—	—	yes	—	—	yes
Deluxe Coupe	—	—	—	yes	yes	yes	—
Sport Coupe	—	—	—	yes	yes	yes	—
Standard Tudor	—	—	—	yes	—	—	yes
Deluxe Tudor	—	—	—	yes	yes	yes	—
Standard Fordor	—	—	—	yes	—	—	yes
Deluxe Fordor	—	—	—	yes	yes	yes	—
Victoria	—	—	—	yes	yes	yes	—
Cabriolet	yes	—	—	—	—	yes	—
Convertible Sedan	yes	—	yes	—	—	yes	—

A 1932 Ford 5-window Coupe customized to tow a mobile radio station illustrates demand for special accessories.

LUGGAGE RACKS

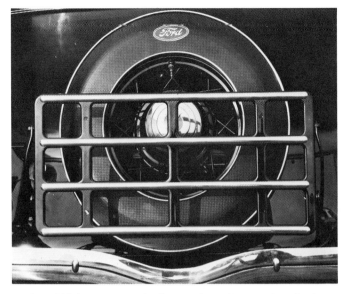

The 1933 luggage rack shown shared stamping designs with the 1929 to 1934 Ford. This car has the accessory 1933 fabric tire cover.

1935 Ford luggage rack

The 1937 luggage rack was the last of this type accessory offered by Ford.

Ford luggage rack in load position

A classy Ford accessory available through 1937 was the luggage rack which attached to the rear bumper. The 1932-34 item was a modification of the Model A rack, utilizing the same stamping but different detailing and side supports. The 1933-34 racks were available with or without chrome-plate scuff bars and the standard finish for racks in all years was black. However, dealers were encouraged by Ford to paint the luggage racks on showroom cars body or wheel color to promote sales.

1936 Ford luggage rack

143

Santa Claus driving a 3-window Coupe in a 1932 dealer Christmas display

Ford dealer's parts department in 1932 featuring a showcase of accessories

Authorized accessories on a 1934 Ford Fordor Sedan

1933-34 Ford accessory display

Featured in the exhibit to the left is an automatic winterfront first offered on a Ford in October, 1932. This replaced the grille and consisted of a system of shutters controlled by a thermostat. In August of that same year appeared the first Ford radio (lower right in the cabinet). These were supplied by Grigsby-Grunow Corp. and had controls which attached to the steering column while the chassis was mounted in the rear floor pan.

While most 1933-34 Ford accessories interchanged, a few such as the greyhound radiator cap (1934 only) did not. In the top photo a Deluxe closed car is shown dressed up with the optional dual windshield wipers, sportlight, and greyhound cap. This car also has hood louvre stripes which indicate that it was specially detailed for show. Accessories pictured above include the unique glove compartment radio, draft deflectors (wind wings), sportlight, and spare wheel (1933) lock.

1933 FORD STANDARDS AND OPTIONS

Engine: *75hp V8 or 50hp 4-cyl*, Transmission: *3-speed manual*, Wheelbase: *112-inches*

CAR COLORS

BODY	STRIPE	FENDERS	DLX WHEELS	★ STD WHEELS
True Black	Vermilion	Black	Vermilion	—
Brewster Green Medium	Silver Gray	Black	Tacoma Cream	—
☆ Duncan Blue	Silver Gray	Black	Tacoma Cream	Black
Emperor Brown Medium	Tacoma Cream	Black	Tacoma Cream	—
☆ Coach Maroon	Vermilion	Black	Vermilion	Black
☆ Old Chester Gray	Tacoma Cream	Black	Tacoma Cream	Black

☆ Standard passenger car color
★ wheels in colors optional at extra cost

INSTRUMENT PANEL

Deluxe models *Burl-grained Walnut in Mahogany shade*,
Standard models *Gray (early cars)*, *Maroon (late cars)*

UPHOLSTERY

	Blk/Brn fine grain genuine Leather	Blk/Brn fine grain artific. Leather	Thorn Brown Mohair	Tan Pin-stripe Broadcloth	Rose Beige Mohair	Brown Pin-stripe Broadcloth	Tan Bedford Cord	Rumble Copra drab fine grain artific. Leather	Rumble Blk/Brn fine grain artific. Leather
Std Phaeton	—	yes	—	—	—	—	—	—	—
Dlx Phaeton	yes	—	—	—	—	—	—	—	—
Std Rdstr	—	yes	—	—	—	—	—	—	yes
Dlx Rdstr	yes	—	—	—	—	—	—	yes	—
Std 5-W Cpe	—	—	yes	yes	—	—	—	—	yes
Dlx 5-W Cpe	—	—	—	—	yes	yes	—	yes	—
Std 3-W Cpe	—	—	yes	yes	—	—	—	yes	—
Dlx 3-W Cpe	—	—	—	—	yes	yes	—	yes	—
Std Tudor	—	—	yes	yes	—	—	—	—	—
Dlx Tudor	—	—	—	—	yes	yes	—	—	—
Std Fordor	—	—	yes	yes	—	—	—	—	—
Dlx Fordor	—	—	—	—	yes	yes	—	—	—
Victoria	—	—	—	—	yes	yes	—	—	—
Cabriolet	yes	—	—	—	—	—	yes	yes	—

1933 Ford with fender spares

1934 Ford with luggage trunk

An option on all 1932-34 Ford cars (except 1932 Deluxe Coupe) at extra cost was the commercial single or dual mount spare wheel and tire. These were installed in welled fenders at the factory. Metal covers were also optional. Available for 1933-34 sedans and phaetons was the bolt-on luggage trunk by Porter. These were popular items and came with bumper extensions for installation.

1934 FORD STANDARDS AND OPTIONS

Engine: *85hp V8 or 50hp (except Victoria) 4-cylinder*
Transmission: *3-speed manual* Wheelbase: *112-inches*

DELUXE CAR COLORS

BODY	STRIPE	FENDERS	WHEELS
Medium Luster Black	*Tacoma Cream*	*Black*	*Tacoma Cream*
☆ *Dearborn Blue*	*Tacoma Cream*	*Dearborn Blue*	*Tacoma Cream*
Cordoba Gray	★ *Tacoma Cream*	*Cordoba Gray*	★★ *Cordoba Gray*
Vineyard Green	☆☆ *Silver Gray*	*Vineyard Green*	☆☆ *Vineyard Green*
Coach Maroon	*Engl. Coach Vermillion*	*Coach Maroon*	*Aurora Red*

☆ not specified for Cabriolet or Victoria
★ also English Coach Vermilion , ★★ also Aurora Red and Tacoma Cream
☆☆ also Tacoma Cream

STANDARD CAR COLORS

Medium Luster Black	*Tacoma Cream*	*Black*	*Black*
Dearborn Blue	*Tacoma Cream*	*Black*	*Black*
Cordoba Gray	*Tacoma Cream*	☆ *Cordoba Gray*	*Black*
Vineyard Green	*Silver Gray*	☆ *Vineyard Green*	*Black*
Coach Maroon	*Eng. Coach Vermilion*	*Black*	*Black*

☆ Black fenders optional. Wheels in colors to match body (all colors) optional

INSTRUMENT PANEL

Deluxe models *Mahogany color with Walnut-grain effect*, Standard models *plain Mahogany color*

UPHOLSTERY

	Copra Drab genuine Leather	Black/ Brown artific. Leather	Rose Beige Mohair	Brown Pin-stripe Broad-cloth	Thorn Brown Mohair	Tan Pin-stripe Broad-cloth	Bed-ford Cord	Rumble Copra Drab fine artific. Leather	Rumble Blk/Brn fine artific. Leather
Std. Phaeton	—	*yes*	—	—	—	—	—	—	—
Dlx. Phaeton	*yes*	—	—	—	—	—	—	—	—
Dlx. Roadster	*yes*	—	—	—	—	—	—	*yes*	—
Std 5-W Cpe	—	—	—	—	*yes*	*yes*	—	—	*yes*
Dlx 5-W Cpe	—	—	*yes*	*yes*	—	—	—	*yes*	—
Dlx 3-W Cpe	—	—	*yes*	*yes*	—	—	—	*yes*	—
Std Tudor	—	—	—	—	*yes*	*yes*	—	—	—
Std Fordor	—	—	—	—	*yes*	*yes*	—	—	—
Victoria	—	—	*yes*	—	—	—	*yes*	—	—
Cabriolet	*yes*	—	—	—	—	—	*yes*	*yes*	—

1933-34 Ford Accessories Listed on Page 150
Ford regarded all of its 1933-34 cars as "Model 40's" and made little distinction between the two years as to add-on accessories. As the items were available they were authorized for both types with few exceptions. Two new accessories developed during this time were the individually styled 8-day clocks available in either the rear view mirror, or installed in the glove compartment door.

1933-34 Ford Glove Compartment Clock

1935 Ford Standard Tudor Sedan, factory-painted for Yellow Cab

SPECIAL PAINT AND FLEET COLORS

Ford's ability to turn out special paint jobs on the assembly line can be appreciated by these shots of a custom-finished Tudor Sedan at the Louisville, Kentucky, plant in 1935.

Beginning in the Model A era, each assembly plant had been equipped with a special commercial paint line to capitalize on fleet sales; and by the mid-30's this was a flourishing department. Paint was stocked in a wide selection of colors, and a corps of skilled maskers, painters, and letterers would work to order turning out jobs as simple as painting a truck in solid Bell Telephone Green, or as elaborate as the two-tone taxi shown here.

Dealers were encouraged to write up such business for the plants, and in 1932 were adding an extra $2.50 to the price of units for "painting the belt moulding on an open cab, closed cab, or panel body in a color other than standard." Other options included the painting of chassis and fenders in special colors.

Fleet buyers were given special privilege, as evidenced by sales instructions sent out in 1934 that there would be "no charge to fleet

148

Taxicab paint design shows range of Ford masking, striping, and lettering skills

Photographed outside the Louisville plant, a freshly painted Yellow Cab offers excess testimony to Ford's special paint shops. Part of a fleet, this car required extensive masking to create the desired effect with the two-tone design merging at random points rather than strictly following body reveals. Non-Ford accessory wheels were another concession to the capture of a fleet order. Painted grille, horn and windshield frame mark the car as a standard model.

owners for painting passenger or commercial bodies a combination of their company colors as long as not more than three colors are to be used on any one body.'' The ''combination of colors'' was further explained as meaning ''painting the belt moulding one color, another color above the belt, and perhaps still another color below the belt.''

As defined by Ford, fleet owners were firms ordering five or more units at one time . . . or national firms that had established fleet discounts.

1932-42 GENUINE FORD OPTIONS AND ACCESSORIES

	1932	1933	1934	1935	1936	1937	1938	1939	1940	1941	1942
Side View Mirror	yes	yes	yes	yes	yes	yes	yes	yes	yes	yes	yes
RH Side View Mirror	—	—	—	—	—	—	—	—	yes	yes	yes
Tandem w/s Wipers	—	(yes)	yes	yes	yes	yes	yes	☆	☆	☆	☆
Sportlight	yes	yes	yes	yes	yes	yes	yes	yes	yes	yes	yes
Dual Taillight	yes	☆	☆	☆	☆	☆	☆	☆	☆	☆	☆
Cowl Lamps	yes	yes	yes	—	—	—	—	—	—	—	—
Road (fog) Lamps	—	—	—	—	—	yes	yes	yes	yes	yes	yes
Locking Gas Cap	—	yes	yes	yes	yes	yes	yes	yes	yes	yes	yes
Glove Comp. Lock	—	(yes)	yes	yes	yes	yes	yes	☆	☆	☆	☆
Seat Covers	—	yes	yes	yes	yes	yes	yes	yes	yes	yes	yes
Radio	yes	yes	yes	yes	yes	yes	yes	yes	yes	yes	yes
Heater	yes	yes	yes	yes	yes	yes	yes	yes	yes	yes	yes
Defroster	—	—	—	yes	yes	yes	yes	yes	yes	yes	yes
Draft Deflectors	yes	yes	yes	yes	yes	yes	yes	☆	☆	☆	
Mirror Clock	—	yes	yes	yes	yes	yes	—	—	—	—	—
Glove Comp. Clock	—	(yes)	yes	yes	yes	yes	yes	yes	yes	yes	yes
Visor-Vanity Mirror	—	—	yes	yes	yes	yes	yes	yes	yes	yes	
Radio foot-control	—	—	—	—	—	—	—	—	—	yes	yes
Hand-brake signal	—	—	—	—	—	—	—	—	—	—	yes
RH Cowl Map Pocket	—	(yes)	yes	—	—	—	—	—	—	—	—
Cigar Lighter	—	yes	yes	yes	yes	yes	yes	☆	☆	☆	☆
Ash Tray	—	yes	yes	—	—	—	—	—	—	—	—

WHEEL EQUIPMENT

	1932	1933	1934	1935	1936	1937	1938	1939	1940	1941	1942
Chrome Wheels	—	(yes)	yes	yes	yes	—	—	—	—	—	—
Wheel Bands	—	(yes)	yes	yes	yes	yes	yes	yes	yes	yes	yes
Deluxe Hubcap	—	—	—	—	yes	yes	yes	yes	yes	yes	—
White Sidewall Tires	—	—	—	yes	yes	yes	yes	yes	yes	yes	yes
Spare Wheel Lock	yes	yes	yes	yes	yes	—	—	—	—	—	—
Spare Tire Cover	yes	yes	☆	☆	☆	—	—	—	—	—	—

FENDER EQUIPMENT

	1932	1933	1934	1935	1936	1937	1938	1939	1940	1941	1942
Welled Fenders	yes	yes	yes	—	—	—	—	—	—	—	—
Fender Mouldings	—	—	—	—	—	—	—	—	—	yes	—

BUMPER EQUIPMENT

	1932	1933	1934	1935	1936	1937	1938	1939	1940	1941	1942
Bumper Guards	—	(yes)	yes	—	—	—	—	—	—	—	—
Center Bumper Guard	—	—	—	—	—	—	yes	yes	yes	yes	yes
Rear Center Guard	—	—	—	—	—	—	—	—	yes	yes	—
Bumper end-Guards	—	—	—	—	—	—	—	—	yes	yes	yes
Gravel Deflector	—	—	—	—	—	—	—	—	yes	yes	☆

TRAVEL EQUIPMENT

	1932	1933	1934	1935	1936	1937	1938	1939	1940	1941	1942
Luggage Rack	yes	yes	yes	yes	yes	yes	—	—	—	—	—
Luggage Trunk	—	(yes)	yes	—	—	—	—	—	—	—	—
Rumble Seat	yes	yes	yes	yes	yes	yes	★	★	—	—	—

DRESS-UP ACCESSORIES

	1932	1933	1934	1935	1936	1937	1938	1939	1940	1941	1942
Deluxe Steering Wheel	—	—	—	[yes]	yes	yes	yes	☆	☆	☆	☆
Greyhound Rad. Cap	—	—	yes	—	—	—	—	—	—	—	—
License Plate Frames	—	(yes)	yes	yes	yes	yes	yes	yes	yes	yes	yes
Fender Shields (Skirts)	—	—	—	—	—	yes	yes	yes	yes	yes	yes

Additional accessories for certain years included Winterfront, Oil Filter, Oil Bath Air Cleaner, Dual Engine Gauges, Governor, Chamois, Bulb and Fuse Kit and Tire Repair Kit.

☆made standard equipment or featured on Deluxe models, ★standard on Convt. Coupe
(yes) 1934 item authorized also for 1933, [yes] 1936 item authorized also for 1935

A Los Angeles Ford dealer sells a spring-colored 1936 Deluxe Fordor Touring Sedan.

SPRING COLORS

"We have selected 'Garnet' as an outstanding Deluxe Ford and Mercury Spring color to dress up dealers' showrooms during the Easter Season," wrote the Ford General Sales Department to dealers February 22, 1940. "This is a temporary additional color . . . and will be discontinued the end of March."

Every Spring for a period of six years, letters such as this made the announcement of another enticing Ford color to add a little freshness to the regular V8 selections on the salesfloor.

It all began informally back in 1934 when Ford Motor Company sent a few scattered dealers models in two-tone or in Silver or Cream as part of the Chicago World's Fair promotions. These bright cars proved so popular in perking up depressed prospects that the following year, with Ford's participation in the San Diego Exposition, three extra "promotional" colors were offered to dealers to supplement their regular 1935 passenger car paint chips. These were Palm Beach Gray, Rust Brown Metallic, and Slate Green.

Then, in the spring of 1936, Ford officially introduced the first of its annual "Spring" or "Easter Colors," which would be tied directly to sales promotion rather than to any particular

Each March from 1936 to 1941, the Ford assembly plants sent dealers a limited number of cars in special colors to boost spring sales. Well-loaded with accessories and targeted for the man looking for the perfect Easter present, the bonny V8's were priced high but sold well. The car being shown above is equipped with double white sidewall tires, wheel bands, side mirror, tandem wipers, and full-chrome grille. We can imagine it in glamorous Desert Sand with Bright Poppy Red pin stripe.

show. Shipped to dealers that year for a widely publicized "Easter Display" were cars specially finished in Desert Sand, Bambalina Blue, Light Fast Maroon, and Armory Green— all with complimenting pin stripes and accessories.

Spring-colored Fords were offered to dealers seasonally between March, 1936, and mid-May, 1941, when the program was discontinued. With Mercurys the special colors were offered beginning March 29, 1939, and discontinued shortly after May 2, 1941.

In selecting colors for both production and seasonal promotion, Ford stylists worked closely with Lincoln, the Company's luxury car division. Such colors as Desert Sand, Bambalina Blue, Brewster Green, and Thorne Brown had been in use on Lincoln cars since the 1920's and adapted very nicely to the classy Ford V8.

151

1935 FORD STANDARDS AND OPTIONS

Engine: *85hp V8,* Transmission: *3-speed manual,* Wheelbase: *112-inches*

DELUXE CAR COLORS

BODY	STRIPE	FENDERS	WHEELS
Med. Luster Black	*Brt. Apple Green*	*Black Japan*	*Med. Apple Green*
Dearborn Blue	*Med. Brt. Poppy Red*	*Dearborn Blue*	*Med. Brt. Poppy Red*
Light Gunmetal	*Brt. Apple Green*	*Light Gunmetal*	*Light Gunmetal*
Cordoba Gray	*Med. Brt. Poppy Red*	*Cordoba Gray*	★ *Cordoba Gray*
Vineyard Green	*Brt. Apple Green*	*Vineyard Green*	★★ *Vineyard Green*
★ or *Medium Poppy Red*	★★ or *Medium Apple Green*		

STANDARD CAR COLORS

Medium Luster Black	*Brt. Apple Green*	*Black Japan*	*Black Japan*
Vineyard Green	*Brt. Apple Green*	*Vineyard Green*	*Black Japan*
Cordoba Gray	*Med. Brt. Poppy Red*	*Cordoba Gray*	*Black Japan*

PROMOTIONAL COLORS

Palm Beach Gray, Rust Brown Metallic, Slate Green

INSTRUMENT PANEL

Deluxe models *Metallic Taupe,* Standard models *Mahogany color*

UPHOLSTERY

	Genuine Leather	Mohair	Taupe stripe Broadcloth	Taupe Wool Suede	Taupe Bedford Cord	Wide Wale Bedford Cord	Rumble Brown artificial Leather
Phaeton	yes	—	—	—	—	—	—
Roadster	yes	—	—	—	—	—	yes
Standard 5-W Coupe	—	—	—	—	—	yes	yes
Deluxe 5-W Coupe	—	yes	yes	—	—	—	yes
Deluxe 3-W Coupe	—	yes	yes	—	—	—	yes
Standard Tudor	—	—	—	—	—	yes	—
Deluxe Tudor	—	yes	yes	—	—	—	—
Standard Fordor	—	—	—	—	—	yes	—
Deluxe Fordor	—	yes	yes	—	—	—	—
Tudor Touring	—	—	—	yes	yes	—	—
Fordor Touring	—	—	—	yes	yes	—	—
Cabriolet	yes	—	—	—	yes	—	yes
Convertible Sedan	yes	—	—	—	yes	—	—

1935 Accessories Listed on Page 150
A rumble seat was available for open and closed Ford V8 Coupe-types from 1932 to 1936 and for the 1937 Roadster and 1938-39 Cabriolets. Generally speaking, this special feature came as standard equipment on the Deluxe Roadsters and Cabriolets and was an option at extra cost on the others. The cushions were always in artificial leather; the side panels were covered with upholstery board; and the floor was finished with a rubber mat.

1935 Ford optional rumble seat

1935 Ford Sport Light

Optional 1932 Ford spare tire cover

1933 Ford spare tire covers

1935 Ford Side View Mirror

1934 Ford spare tire cover and lock

1935 Ford spare tire cover and lock

1935 Ford Ash Tray Radio

1936 Ford spare tire cover

All 1932-36 Ford passenger cars had the spare mounted on the rear (excepting those with side mounts), and these were figured into the factory price as accessories along with front and rear bumpers. The spare tire covers were also accessories, and in 1932 were sold by the dealer. In that year three types were offered: fabric with metal edging, metal with black inner and chrome outer ring, and a black band with a stainless trim moulding. The 1933 Standard models were factory-equipped with a fabric stretch-on-cover, while Deluxe cars had a two-piece black metal cover with stainless mouldings on the faceplate and band. A fabric cover with metal edging was also available as an option. Quite often these were switched at the dealership to make a sale. The 1934-36 Fords had factory-equipped tire covers in body colors with a stainless trim ring on the faceplate.

1936 FORD STANDARDS AND OPTIONS

Engine: *85 hp V8*, Transmission: *3-speed manual*, Wheelbase: *112-inches*

☆DELUXE CAR COLORS

BODY	STRIPE	FENDERS	☆ ☆ WHEELS
Medium Luster Black	*Bright Apple Green*	*Black Japan*	*Black Japan*
Gun Metal Gray	*Med. Bright Poppy Red*	*Gun Metal Gray*	*Gun Metal Gray*
Gray Vineyard Green	*Silver*	*Gray Vineyard Green*	*Gray Vineyard Green*
Washington Blue	*Tacoma Green*	*Washington Blue*	*Washington Blue*
Cordoba Tan	*Med. Bright Poppy Red*	*Cordoba Tan*	*Cordoba Tan*

☆ also Sedan Delivery

☆ ☆ Red, Cream, or Apple Green wheels optional on all passenger cars and matched to Medium Bright Poppy Red, Tacoma Cream, or Bright Apple Green stripe

STANDARD CAR COLORS

Black	*Bright Apple Green*	*Black Japan*	*Black Japan*
Gun Metal Gray	*Med. Bright Poppy Red*	*Gun Metal Gray*	*Black Japan*
★*Washington Blue*	*Tacoma Green*	*Washington Blue*	*Black Japan*

★available after January 31, 1936

SPRING COLORS

Bambalina Blue	*Tacoma Cream*	*Bambalina Blue*	*Bambalina Blue*
Light Fast Maroon	*Gold*	*Light Fast Maroon*	*Light Fast Maroon*
Armory Green	*Silver*	*Armory Green*	*Armory Green*
Desert Sand	*Bright Poppy Red*	*Desert Sand*	*Desert Sand*

STATION WAGON COLOR

Cordoba Tan	*no stripe*	*Cordoba Tan*	*Cordoba Tan*

INSTRUMENT PANEL

Deluxe models *Benton Gray Metallic or Walnut Grain*, Standard models *Mahogany Grain*

UPHOLSTERY

	Brown fine Colonial Grain Genuine Leather	Taupe Wide Wale Cord	Taupe Bedford Cord	Taupe Mohair	Taupe Pinstripe Broadcloth	*Rumble* Brown artificial Leather
Phaeton	yes	—	—	—	—	—
Roadster	yes	—	—	—	—	yes
Std. 5-W Coupe	—	yes	—	—	—	yes
Dlx. 5-W Coupe	—	—	—	yes	yes	yes
Dlx. 3-W Coupe	—	—	—	yes	yes	yes
Std. Tudor	—	yes	—	—	—	—
Dlx. Tudor	—	—	yes	yes	yes	—
Std. Fordor	—	yes	—	—	—	—
Dlx. Fordor	—	—	yes	yes	yes	—
Tudor Touring	—	—	yes	yes	yes	—
Fordor Touring	—	—	yes	yes	yes	—
Cabriolet	yes	—	yes	—	—	yes
Convert. Sedan	yes	—	yes	—	—	—

1936 Ford Accessories Listed on Page 150

Dealers ordered customer's cars from the assembly plants in requested colors and with accessories sold in "groups." The three basic groups for 1936 ranged from ten items installed for an extra $72, to Radio, Dual Wipers, and Vanity Mirror for $48. Accessories like those to the right were also commonly installed at the dealership.

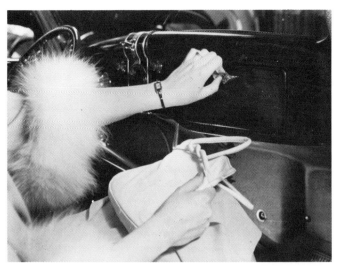
1936 Glove Compartment Lock

1936 Side View Mirror

1936 Seat Covers

1936 Sportlight, Dual Wipers, and Draft Deflectors

Accessory white wall tires on a 1936 3-window Coupe

1936 Radiator Winterfront

1937 FORD STANDARDS AND OPTIONS

Engine: *85hp V8 or 60hp (Standard body types only) V8*
Transmission: *3-speed manual* Wheelbase: *112-inches*

CAR COLORS

BODY	STRIPE	FENDERS	WHEELS
☆ *Black*	*Tacoma Cream*	*Black*	*Black*
☆ *Washington Blue*	*Tacoma Cream*	*Washington Blue*	*Washington Blue*
☆ *Gull Gray*	*Bright Vermilion*	*Gull Gray*	*Gull Gray*
Bright Vineyard Green	*Silver*	*Bright Vineyard Green*	*Bright Vineyard Green*
Autumn Brown	*Tacoma Cream*	*Autumn Brown*	*Autumn Brown*
Coach Maroon Bright	*Gold*	*Coach Maroon Bright*	*Coach Maroon Bright*

☆ Deluxe color which is also specified for Standard cars

SPRING COLORS

Turquoise Blue	*Silver*	*Turquoise Blue*	*Silver*
Dalmation Green	*Logan Cream*	*Dalmation Green*	*Logan Cream*
Silver Wing Gray	*Pomegranate Red*	*Silver Wing Gray*	*Pomegranate Red*
Adobe Tan	*Chinese Red*	*Adobe Tan*	*Chinese Red*

STATION WAGON

Autumn Brown	*no stripe*	*Autumn Brown*	*Autumn Brown*

INSTRUMENT PANEL

Deluxe models *straight grain American Walnut*, Standard models *burl grain Mahogany*

UPHOLSTERY

	Tan Antique finished Leather	*Rumble artific. Leather*	Taupe Bedford Cord	Gray Mohair	Light Taupe Mohair	Taupe Broadcloth	Flat Wale Cord	Light Taupe Broadcloth	Taupe Mohair
Phaeton	yes	—	—	—	—	—	—	—	—
Roadster	yes	yes	—	—	—	—	—	—	—
Std 5-W Cpe	—	—	—	—	—	yes	—	—	yes
Dlx 5-W Cpe	—	—	—	yes	—	—	yes	—	—
Club Coupe	—	—	—	yes	—	—	yes	—	—
Std Tudor	—	—	—	—	—	yes	—	—	yes
Dlx Tudor	—	—	—	—	yes	—	—	yes	—
Std Fordor	—	—	—	—	—	yes	—	—	yes
Dlx Fordor	—	—	—	—	yes	—	—	yes	—
Std Tudor Tour	—	—	—	—	—	yes	—	—	yes
Dlx Tudor Tour	—	—	—	—	yes	—	—	yes	—
Std Fordor Tour	—	—	—	—	—	yes	—	—	yes
Dlx Fordor Tour	—	—	—	—	yes	—	—	yes	—
Cabriolet	yes	yes	yes	—	—	—	—	—	—
Club Cabriolet	yes	—	yes	—	—	—	—	—	—
Convt. Sedan	yes	—	yes	—	—	—	—	—	—

1937 Ford Accessories Listed on Page 150
New to the Ford accessory line for 1937 were fender skirts.
These were locked on for protection with a stylized chrome
nut. Road lamps were also new for 1937.

1937 Winterfront

1937 Road Lamp

1937 Side View Mirror

1937 Rear Fender Shields (skirts)

Factory-installed artificial leather upholstery in a 1938 Ford police car

ALL-LEATHER INTERIORS

An option seldom exercised in the purchase of a Ford V8 coupe or sedan was the choice of leather upholstery for a few dollars more.

Actually, this type interior in closed cars was first offered on 1932 Fords for export, and from that experience was adapted to sales at home as well. Regarded with indifference by Americans who clearly preferred the warmth and coziness of their familiar mohair or broadcloth interiors, the leather option's only takers seemed to be the occasional traveling salesman, veterinarian, cab driver or police department, which found the durability to their liking. Prices for this type interior ranged from an extra $10 on the 1932 Deluxe Coupe to $25 on the Fordor.

These early experiments with leather interiors in closed cars would form the basis for a durable upholstery alternative leading up to the colorful vinyls in Fords today. However, in the 30's it was considered second-rate styling, and dealers were cautioned by the branch plants that the option was to be handled discreetly as they did not want a proliferation of leather jobs. This was spelled out emphatically in a sales letter dated January 22, 1934, which stated, "We do

The Ford leather interior option is nicely illustrated in this photo taken at the Louisville plant December 13, 1937. When genuine leather was specified in closed cars it was used on the seat cushions and backs, cushion facings, and arm rest trim, with artificial leather on the sidewalls and headlining. As this was a police car the interior was specified in artificial leather throughout. A split seat back in the rear compartment permitted entry of a folded stretcher stowed in the trunk.

not want to encourage the specification of genuine leather upholstery for types on which it is not standard equipment but to prevent the loss of retail business, we will furnish genuine leather upon special request . . ."

That letter went on to complain that, ". . . there might be instances when purchasers will demand artificial leather throughout in the standard types . . . in which case it will be furnished at an extra charge of $7.50."

From statements such as this, photographic evidence, and surviving examples, together with Ford's liberal commercial policies and bid for business, it is reasonable to assume that the genuine or artificial leather options were available right on through WWII production.

A 1938 Ford Deluxe Fordor equipped with accessory fender skirts, wheel covers, wind wings, road lamp, and white sidewall tires. A complete listing of accessories for this model may be found on page 150.

1938 FORD STANDARDS AND OPTIONS

Engine: *85hp V8 or 60hp (Standard body types only) V8*
Transmission: *3-speed manual* Wheelbase: 112-inches

CAR COLORS

Entire body, fenders, and wheels. No pin stripe.
*Black, Washington Blue, Bright Vineyard Green, Bright Coach Maroon,
Gull Gray, ☆Wren Tan Dark, Dartmouth Green*
☆ also Station Wagon color

SPRING COLORS

Entire body, fenders, and wheels. No pin stripe.
Dove Gray, Avon Blue

INSTRUMENT PANEL

Deluxe models *straight grain American Walnut*, Standard models *burl grain Mahogany*

UPHOLSTERY

	Tan Antique Leather	Taupe Bedford Cord	Striped Mohair	Taupe Broadcloth	Standard Mohair
Phaeton	*yes*	—	—	—	—
Std 5-W Coupe	—	—	—	*yes*	*yes*
Dlx 5-W Coupe	—	—	*yes*	*yes*	—
Club Coupe	—	—	*yes*	*yes*	—
Dlx Tudor	—	—	*yes*	*yes*	—
Std Tudor	—	—	—	*yes*	*yes*
Dlx Fordor	—	—	*yes*	*yes*	—
Std Fordor	—	—	—	*yes*	*yes*
Convt Coupe	*yes*	*yes*	—	—	—
Convt Club Coupe	*yes*	*yes*	—	—	—
Convt Sedan	*yes*	*yes*	—	—	—

1939 FORD STANDARDS AND OPTIONS

Engine: *85hp V8 or 60hp (Std body type only) V8,*
Transmission: *3-speed manual,* Wheelbase: *112-inches*

DELUXE CAR COLORS

Entire body, fenders and wheels
Black, Jefferson Blue, Dartmouth Green, Gull Gray, Folkestone Gray, Coach Maroon Bright

STANDARD CAR COLORS

Entire body and fenders, wheels *Black* as standard equipment but
available in body colors at extra cost.
Black, Jefferson Blue, Gull Gray

SPRING COLOR

Entire body, fenders, and wheels
Cloud Mist Gray

INSTRUMENT PANEL

Deluxe models *Golden grain Mahogany,* Standard models *Antique grain Mahogany*

UPHOLSTERY

	Russett Leather	Taupe Broadcloth	Green Striped Mohair	Taupe Mohair
Std 5-W Coupe	—	yes	—	—
Deluxe 5-W Coupe	—	yes	yes	—
Standard Tudor	—	yes	—	yes
Deluxe Tudor	—	yes	yes	—
Standard Fordor	—	yes	—	yes
Deluxe Fordor	—	yes	yes	—
Convertible Coupe	yes	—	—	—
Convertible Sedan	yes	—	—	—

1939 MERCURY STANDARDS AND OPTIONS

Engine: *95hp V8,* Transmission: *3-speed manual,* Wheelbase: *116-inches*

COLORS

Wheels and fenders finished in body color.
*Black, Jefferson Blue, Gull Gray, Coach Maroon Bright, Dartmouth Green,
Folkestone Gray, Mercury Blue Metallic, Tropical Green*

★SPRING COLORS

Cloud Mist Gray, Claret Maroon
★ offered March 29, 1939

INSTRUMENT PANEL

Gray-Tan finish

UPHOLSTERY

	Red Genuine Leather	Russett Genuine Leather	Taupe Stripe Broadcloth	Taupe Bedford Cord
Sedan	—	—	yes	yes
Town Sedan	—	—	yes	yes
Sedan Coupe	—	—	yes	yes
Sport Convertible	yes	yes	—	—

1939 Ford and Mercury accessories shown above include Wheel Covers, Spot Light, Road Lamp, Side View Mirror, Wind Wings, Center Bumper Guards, Locking Gas Cap, Wheel Trim Rings, Heater and Defroster. Others are listed on page 150.

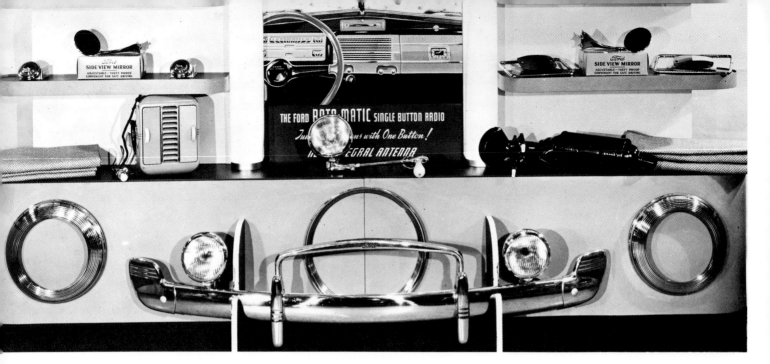

This 1940 Ford accessory display includes optional hot water and hot air heater, spot light, road lamps, wheel trim rings and covers, center grille guard, and bumper end guards. A non-Ford item, first offered in 1933, was the Columbia 2-speed rear axle that was installed by the dealer. More accessories are listed on page 150.

1940 MERCURY STANDARDS AND OPTIONS

Engine: *95hp V8*, Transmission: *3-speed manual*, Wheelbase: *116-inches*

COLORS

Wheels and fenders finished in body color.
Black, Cloud Mist Gray, Lyon Blue, Folkestone Gray, Sahara Sand,
Yosemite Green, Mandarin Maroon, Acadia Green

★ SPRING COLORS

Wheels and fenders finished in body color.
Garnet, Cotswold Gray
★ Temporary colors only available during the month of March, 1940

☆ TWO-TONE COLORS

BODY	FENDERS	WHEELS
Folkestone Gray	*Black*	*Folkestone Gray*
Folkestone Gray	*Mandarin Maroon*	*Folkestone Gray*
Mandarin Maroon	*Folkestone Gray*	*Mandarin Maroon*
Cloud Mist Gray	*Acadia Green*	*Cloud Mist Gray*

☆ available May 3, 1940

INSTRUMENT PANEL

Combination *Silver*, and *Blue plastic*

UPHOLSTERY

	Saddle Brown Gen. Leather	Antique Red Gen. Leather	Two-tone Bedford Cord	Blue-Gray Barkweave Broadcloth
Sedan	—	—	*yes*	*yes*
Town Sedan	—	—	*yes*	*yes*
Sedan Coupe	—	—	*yes*	*yes*
Sport Convertible	*yes*	*yes*	—	—
Convertible Sedan	*yes*	*yes*	—	—

1940 FORD STANDARDS AND OPTIONS

Engine: *85hp V8 or 60hp (Standard body types only) V8*
Transmission: *3-speed manual,* Wheelbase: *112-inches*

DELUXE CAR COLORS

Entire body, fenders, and wheels.
Black, Lyon Blue, Cloud Mist Gray, Folkestone Gray,
Yosemite Green, Mandarin Maroon, Acadia Green

STANDARD CAR COLORS

Entire body and fenders. Wheels black as standard equipment but
wheels in body colors optional at extra cost.
Black, Lyon Blue, Cloud Mist Gray

SPRING COLOR *Garnet*

☆TWO-TONE COLORS

BODY	FENDERS	GRILLE SIDES	WHEELS
Folkestone Gray	*Black*	*Black*	*Folkestone Gray*
Folkestone Gray	*Mandarin Maroon*	*Mandarin Maroon*	*Folkestone Gray*
Mandarin Maroon	*Folkestone Gray*	*Folkestone Gray*	*Mandarin Maroon*
Cloud Mist Gray	*Acadia Green*	*Acadia Green*	*Cloud Mist Gray*

☆ available beginning May 3, 1940 on all accessory-equipped Ford passenger units

INSTRUMENT PANEL

Deluxe models two-tone combination with *Monaida Maroon* upper section
and *Copper Sand Metallic* lower section, Standard models *Briarwood Brown*

UPHOLSTERY

	Brown genuine Leather	Red genuine Leather	artific. Leather	Deluxe Mohair	Standard ★Mohair	Deluxe Broadcloth	Standard Broadcloth
Std Bus Coupe	—	—	—	—	yes	—	yes
Dlx Bus Coupe	—	—	—	yes	—	yes	—
Std 5-W Coupe	—	—	—	—	yes	—	—
Dlx 5-W Coupe	—	—	—	yes	—	—	—
Std Tudor Sedan	—	—	—	—	yes	—	yes
Dlx Tudor Sedan	—	—	—	yes	—	yes	—
Std Fordor Sedan	—	—	—	—	yes	—	yes
Dlx Fordor Sedan	—	—	—	yes	—	yes	—
Convertible Coupe	yes	yes	—	—	—	—	—
Dlx Station Wagon	yes	—	—	—	—	—	—
Std Station Wagon	—	—	yes	—	—	—	—

★ optional at extra cost on 60hp models

1940 Ford Tudor Sedan with optional two-tone paint

Designed to liven up Spring sales, the two-tone color scheme offered as an option on 1940 Fords garnered little general interest. This rare photo shows a Tudor in combination *Folkestone Gray* fenders and *Mandarin Maroon* body. Note how the grille sides were also painted fender color.

1941 FORD STANDARDS AND OPTIONS

Engine: *90hp V8 or 90hp 6-cylinder* Transmission: *3-speed manual* Wheelbase: *114-inches*

SUPER DELUXE CAR COLORS

BODY AND FENDERS	WHEELS	WHEEL STRIPE
Black	*Black*	*Vermilion*
Harbor Gray	*Harbor Gray*	*Vermilion*
Mayfair Maroon	*Mayfair Maroon*	*Vermilion*
Palisade Gray	*Palisade Gray*	*Silver Gray*
Lochaven Green	*Lochaven Green*	*Silver Gray*
Cayuga Blue	*Cayuga Blue*	*Silver Gray*

DELUXE AND SPECIAL ★ CAR COLORS

★ *Black*	*Black*	*no stripe*
★ *Harbor Gray*	*Black*	*no stripe*
Cayuga Blue	*Black*	*no stripe*
Lochaven Green	*Black*	*no stripe*
★ *Palisade Gray*	*Black*	*no stripe*
Harbor Gray	*Black*	*no stripe*

SPRING COLORS

Florentine Blue	*Florentine Blue*	*Silver Gray*
Seminole Brown	*Seminole Brown*	*Vermilion*

★ SUPER DELUXE TWO-TONE COLORS

BODY	FENDERS	LOWER DOOR FLARES	WHEELS
Harbor Gray	*Lochaven Green*	*Lochaven Green*	*Lochaven Green*
Harbor Gray	*Palisade Gray*	*Palisade Gray*	*Palisade Gray*
Harbor Gray	*Mayfair Maroon*	*Mayfair Maroon*	*Mayfair Maroon*
Harbor Gray	*Cayuga Blue*	*Cayuga Blue*	*Cayuga Blue*

★ each of these colors is reversible for a total of 8 combinations.

PASSENGER CAR INSTRUMENT PANEL

Super Deluxe models *Kelobra grain*, Deluxe models *Ebony grain*

UPHOLSTERY

	Tan genuine Leather	Blue genuine Leather	Red genuine Leather	Light or Dark Tan artific. Leather	Taupe Chevron patterned Mohair	Bedford and Broadcloth weave	Boucle Cloth	Gray Taupe patterned Mohair	Striped Broadcloth
Super Dlx Sed Cpe	—	—	—	—	*yes*	*yes*	—	—	—
Dlx 5-W Coupe	—	—	—	—	—	—	—	*yes*	*yes*
Spec. 5-W Coupe	—	—	—	—	—	—	*yes*	—	—
Dlx. Tudor Sedan	—	—	—	—	—	—	—	*yes*	*yes*
Super Dlx Tudor	—	—	—	—	*yes*	*yes*	—	—	—
Spec. Tudor Sedan	—	—	—	—	—	—	*yes*	—	—
Dlx Fordor Sedan	—	—	—	—	—	—	—	*yes*	*yes*
Super Dlx Fordor Sedan	—	—	—	—	*yes*	*yes*	—	—	—
Spec Fordor Sedan	—	—	—	—	—	—	*yes*	—	—
Super Dlx Convert	*yes*	*yes*	*yes*	—	—	—	—	—	—
Super Dlx Station Wag	*yes*	—	—	—	—	—	—	—	—
Deluxe Station Wagon	—	—	—	*yes*	—	—	—	—	—

1941 Ford accessory display. A listing of Ford items is on page 150

1941 MERCURY STANDARDS AND OPTIONS

Engine: *95hp V8*, Transmission: *3-speed manual*, Wheelbase: *118-inches*

COLORS

Wheels body color with *Vermilion* stripe except that *Silver Gray* is used with *Lochaven Green* and
Palisade Gray body colors
*Black, Harbor Gray, Cayuga Blue, Lochaven Green, Mayfair Maroon,
Palisade Gray, Capri Blue, Cotswold Gray*

SPRING COLOR *Florentine Blue*

★ TWO-TONE COLORS

BODY & HOOD	FENDERS	LOWER DOOR FLARES	WHEELS
Harbor Gray	*Lochaven Green*	*Lochaven Green*	*Lochaven Green*
Harbor Gray	*Palisade Gray*	*Palisade Gray*	*Palisade Gray*
Harbor Gray	*Cotswold Gray*	*Cotswold Gray*	*Cotswold Gray*
Harbor Gray	*Mayfair Maroon*	*Mayfair Maroon*	*Mayfair Maroon*
Harbor Gray	*Cayuga Blue*	*Cayuga Blue*	*Cayuga Blue*
Harbor Gray	*Capri Blue*	*Capri Blue*	*Capri Blue*

★ each of these colors is reversible with *Harbor Gray* for 12 possible combinations

INSTRUMENT PANEL

Combination *Rosemont Beige* and *Gray Elm Grain* finish

UPHOLSTERY

	Tan Leather	Red Leather	Blue Leather	Broad-cloth	Bedford Cord	☆Broad-cloth	☆Bedford Cord
Sedan	—	—	—	yes	yes	—	—
Town Sedan	—	—	—	—	—	yes	yes
Sedan Coupe	—	—	—	yes	yes	yes	yes
5-W Coupe	—	—	—	yes	yes	yes	yes
Convertible	yes	yes	yes	—	—	—	—
Station Wagon	yes	yes	yes	—	—	—	—

☆with *Blue* or *Sand*-colored buttons, or *Blue* leather (coupes only) welt

1942 FORD STANDARDS AND OPTIONS

Engine: *90hp V8 or 90hp 6-cyl*, Transmission: *3-speed manual*, Wheelbase: *114-inches*

CAR COLORS

Entire body, fenders, and wheels. No two-tones or spring colors available.
*Florentine Blue, Newcastle Gray, Niles Blue-Green, Fathom Blue,
Moselle Maroon, Village Green, Phoebe Gray, Black*

INSTRUMENT PANEL

Super Deluxe models *Sequoia grain*, Deluxe models *Crackle Mahogany grain*,
Special models *Kelobra wood grain*

UPHOLSTERY

	Golden Tan genuine Leather	Dark Red genuine Leather	Dark Blue genuine Leather	Brown artific. Leather	Deluxe Mohair	Super Deluxe Mohair	Broadcloth	Deluxe Broadcloth	Super Deluxe Broadcloth
Dlx Coupe w/aux. seats	—	—	—	—	*yes*	—	—	*yes*	—
Super Dlx Sedan Coupe	—	—	—	—	—	*yes*	—	—	*yes*
Dlx 5-W Coupe	—	—	—	—	*yes*	—	—	*yes*	—
Super Dlx 5-W Coupe	—	—	—	—	—	*yes*	—	—	*yes*
Special 5-W Coupe	—	—	—	—	—	—	*yes*	—	—
Dlx Tudor Sedan	—	—	—	—	*yes*	—	—	*yes*	—
Super Dlx Tudor	—	—	—	—	—	*yes*	—	—	*yes*
Special Tudor Sedan	—	—	—	—	—	—	*yes*	—	—
Dlx Fordor Sedan	—	—	—	—	*yes*	—	—	*yes*	—
Super Dlx Fordor	—	—	—	—	—	*yes*	—	—	*yes*
Special Fordor	—	—	—	—	—	—	*yes*	—	—
Super Dlx Convert	*yes*	*yes*	*yes*	—	—	—	—	—	—
Dlx Station Wagon	—	—	—	*yes*	—	—	—	—	—
Super Dlx Station Wagon	*yes*	—	—	—	—	—	—	—	—

1942 Ford Accessories Listed on Page 150

1942 MERCURY STANDARDS AND OPTIONS

Engine: *100hp V8*, Transmission: *3-speed manual*, or *Liquamatic Drive*, Wheelbase: *118-inches*

COLORS

*Florentine Blue, Newcastle Gray, Niles Blue-Green, Fathom Blue,
Moselle Maroon, Village Green, Phoebe Gray, Black*

INSTRUMENT PANEL

Light Silver Walnut Grain or *Mahogany Sequoia Grain*

UPHOLSTERY

	Tan Genuine Leather	Red Genuine Leather	Blue Genuine Leather	Blue/Tan Striped Broadcloth	Tan Striped Bedford Cloth
Sedan	—	—	—	*yes*	*yes*
Town Sedan	—	—	—	*yes*	*yes*
Sedan Coupe	—	—	—	*yes*	*yes*
5-W Coupe	—	—	—	*yes*	*yes*
Club Convertible	*yes*	*yes*	*yes*	—	—
Station Wagon	*yes*	*yes*	*yes*	—	—

Girls wave to Ford-based sailors from their new 1941 "two-tone" Mercury Convertible.

TWO-TONE COLORS

Black fenders, regardless of body color, were standard on all Fords before 1934. Traditionally, the fenders and related sheet metal were dipped in stock black enamel and sent through baking ovens before finally arriving at the assembly line to join a standard all-black chassis. Meanwhile, bodies were being finished on another line, and when eased onto the unit in a contrasting color created, in effect, a Ford in "two-tones."

This practice endured until introduction of the 1934 models when new painting methods allowed fenders to come through along with the bodies in the full variety of colors. While solid-colored Fords had come of fashion, this did not mean the end to cars in two-tones. Orders still dribbled in to assembly plants for black fenders on retail models, as well as for units for show and commercial use.

It wasn't until the 1940 models that Ford Motor Company looked at two-toning from a promotional viewpoint, and for the first time actually specified four optional colors of fenders on contrasting bodies. This unusual styling offer was announced May 3, 1940, when the company notified its assembly plants that it was "satis-

Remembered but rarely seen, the 1940-41 Fords and Mercurys in two-tone color combinations met little success in a conservative pre-war market. On 1940 Fords fenders and grille sides were painted one color, with the body in another shade. Like the car above, 1941's had the body and hood finished in one color with fenders, wheels, and the flared section above the running boards painted another. Each of the 1941 combinations was reversible.

factory to furnish dealers with Ford and Mercury units painted with special color combinations when equipped with our various accessories."

Fords and Mercurys in two-tones were intended to help lagging sales but, even at the nominal $5 extra for the color option, met general indifference. Most buyers found the combinations a bit garish compared to stock selections, and few were sold. Despite the dull reception and the custom work required in assembly, two-tone styling was again offered to Ford and Mercury buyers for 1941. This time there was a choice of 8 color combinations on the Ford Super Deluxe, and 12 on the Mercurys. But then in May, 1941, with a lackluster response and the discontinuance of Harbor Gray as the base shade for both cars, the two-tone program was quietly suspended.

The first post-War Fords on display at the Louisville, Kentucky, plant

EIGHT

Young Henry's Post-war Cars

FORD was the first U.S. auto maker to get back into post-World War II civilian car production; and at Louisville, Kentucky, Stan Corley of radio station WINN broadcast the news of the first car off the line at the big assembly plant in his city. "Production of 1946 Fords began here today in Louisville," reported Corley in his afternoon summary of August 21, 1945. "Contrary to general opinion, this is not a stop-gap model, hurriedly produced. It contains more mechanical improvements than were included in many previous models and is described by Company officials as the smartest Ford ever built. And you can take my word for it, it is a fine car. I had the pleasure of driving the second one off the line this afternoon. *And that's the news to air time!*"

The Lousiville plant was the third of Ford's 12 active facilities to begin peacetime production, after the ones at Dearborn, Michigan, and Edgewater, New Jersey. Louisville Mayor Wilson Wyatt drove the first 1946 Ford off the line in his city and voiced the feelings of thousands of war-weary Kentuckians and Americans alike when he beamed, "It sure makes me feel peace is really here— to drive a new car again."

His sentiments were echoed by regional Ford dealers who sent the Louisville plant manager letters of praise following a new model preview in his showroom that afternoon. "Good job on the 1946 line," wrote the dealer in Franklin, Tennessee. "But get those boys on the job so we can have some! I am one of your youngest dealers, just back from three years overseas." The dealer in Danville, Kentucky, wrote, "attended the preview yesterday. Highly inspirational. Car far above expectations!"

Considering the scarcity of raw materials and the youthful leadership of Henry Ford II, Ford Motor Company miraculously produced America's first post-War cars— even before the surrender of Japan. In the photos opposite taken August 21, 1945, district dealers preview the new cars and trucks at the Louisville, Kentucky, assembly plant.

Backed by the up-beat "Ford in Your Future" advertising slogan, the new Fords held great promise indeed. They were beautifully streamlined with a new front-end treatment, and there was a wide selection of body types and the choice of the new 100hp or the six-cylinder engine. Unfortunately it would be some months before dealers could get enough cars to satisfy even a small part of the demand, since there were still material shortages, government restrictions and labor problems hampering production.

Ford Motor Company had changed considerably during the war. Edsel Ford had died following a short illness in 1943. His eldest son, Henry Ford II, had been recalled from the Navy to aid his grandfather in managing the Company, and the once-matchless industrial organization was in disarray.

Young Henry Ford II is given credit for leading the Company out of the confusion. In quick succession he brought out the new 1946 Ford-Mercury-Lincoln models, while at the same time reorganizing and planning a major retooling for a new series of cars and trucks. The face-lifted 1947 models were introduced in April of that year— the same week Henry Ford died at his home in Dearborn at the grand age of 83.

Making their entrance so late in the model year, the 1947 Fords and Mercurys were met with little fanfare, since it was still a booming seller's market. Virtually the same as the previous models except for cosmetics, the 1947's sold briskly and later that fall were designated 1948 models— again with minor improvements.

Henry Ford II had intended to bring out what we now know as the 1949 Fords in 1948 and for that reason the post-War series was extended a few extra months until the revolutionary new models were ready to take a bow. At final tally the skillfully marketed 1946-48 cars were a smashing success and laid the foundation for the Company's great comeback in the booming 50's.

16,359　　　　　　　1946 Ford Super Deluxe Convertible Club Coupe

Two country girls discuss the features of a new 1946 Ford Convertible. It was the well-connected or top-priority American who was able to buy one of these sport models during the first deliveries. Less than 5 per cent of the 1946 passenger car production was allocated to convertibles— and only 3 per cent in 1947-48. Prospective purchasers were put on long waiting lists until factory output finally caught up with the demand, which had built up over the duration of the war.

Poised as though it is ready to crash out of the showroom and take to the street, a 1947 Ford Convertible awaits a spirited driver at the Tom Boyd dealership in Dearborn, Michigan, July 19, 1947. Just such a deal may be in the making in the lower photo as a young prospect shows his sweetheart how to find the gas pedal. The salesman stands by to write up the ticket which would amount to about $1500 plus the incidentals. Cars that were still on the floor after November 1, 1947, were redesignated 1948 models since the features were nearly identical.

All signals are green, and this Ford beauty is ready to go!

22,159
12,033 (1948)

1947 Ford Super Deluxe Convertible Club Coupe

An extremely rare 1946 Mercury Sportsman for sale in a Detroit showroom

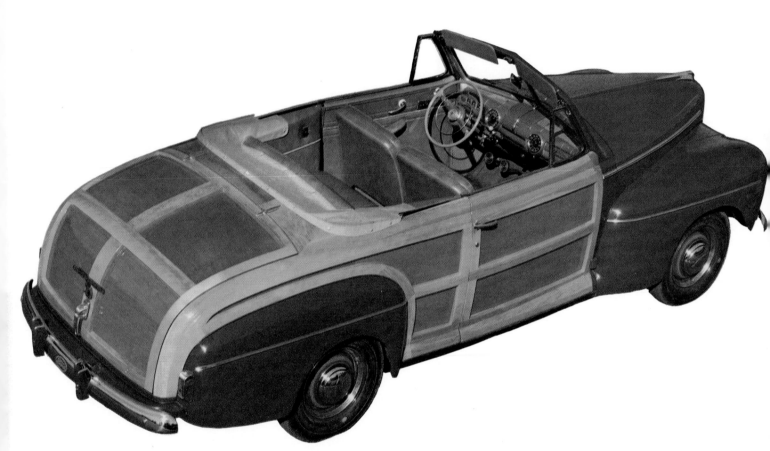

723
2,774 (1947 model)

28 (1948 model)

1946 Ford Super Deluxe Sportsman Convertible Coupe

One of the most distinctive body types ever produced by Ford Motor Company, the Sportsman was conceived by stylists to fill the need for a classy model somewhere between the Station Wagon and Convertible. Ford models were produced 1946 through 1948 while just a small number of the Mercurys were made in 1946— to make it one of the rarest production automobiles of all time. The Sportsman had the same automatic "Motor-Lift" top and seating arrangement as the club convertibles but featured natural wood exterior finish panels built over the steel body framework. The hardwood Maple and Mahogany panels were intricate enough but the large rear deck lid was a masterpiece of bent, dove-tailed, and finger-jointed

craftsmanship. The interiors were richly upholstered in leather and all models were equipped with push-button, hydraulically operated windows.

At the right a salesman talks with a lady prospect in a Dearborn showroom September 16, 1947. In the foreground is one of the low-production Sportsman models which quite often went begging for buyers. Handsome as the richly varnished cars were, many customers feared they might become a real maintenance problem. The 1947 Ford model was priced $200 higher than the conventional convertible which sold for $1436.

172

200   1946 Mercury Sportsman Convertible Coupe

A 1947 Ford Sportsman and Fordor Sedan on display at Stuart Wilson Ford in Dearborn, Michigan

1947 Mercury Convertible in shop for service

Set apart from the Ford line by its streamlined fender side mouldings, wider hood, and bold die-cast grille, the post-War Mercurys gave the impression of more power and substance. The grille on 1946 models was painted, while that of the slightly modified 1947-48 was chrome-plate. Another exterior difference between model years was the hood side moulding treatment. Notice the short moulding and ''Mercury'' nameplate of the 1947-48 design on the car below, versus the hood trim on the earlier car at the left.

6,044   1946 Mercury Convertible Club Coupe

10,221
7,586 (1948)   1947 Mercury Convertible Coupe

1947 Mercury closed car instrument panel

1946 Ford closed car interior

Massive center design characterized the 1946-48 Mercury instrument panel. The Ford panel was more conservative. Both types utilized large clock-type speedometer and in- struments paired with a dominant center radio speaker grille. The Mercury shown here has been equipped with accessory spotlight.

The 1946-48 Ford-Mercury Convertibles (1947 Ford shown) were upholstered in sporty fabrics.

1947-48 Ford Wagon rear details

The outstanding 1946-48 Ford and Mercury Station Wagons would be the last of the full wood-bodied types produced. Indicative of the fabled Iron Mountain craftsmanship is the interior to the left, showing the match of wood grains, hardware, and fabrics to perfection. Seats in the Ford models for these years came in Tan leather while the buyer had a choice of Tan, Red, or Gray genuine leather in the more expensive Mercurys. Instrument panels in the Fords were Maplewood Grain, In the Mercurys they were darker in simulated Walnut Wood Grain. Station Wagon owners would learn to take the Owner's Manual advice and never wax the wood body. The best way to maintain the original lustre is by cleaning the wood surfaces with a damp chamois and by periodic application of genuine varnish (no plastics).

Superbly finished 1947 Ford Station Wagon interior

8,912
16,104 (1947 model)

1948 Ford Super Deluxe Station Wagon

16,960   1946 Ford Super Deluxe Station Wagon

2,797   1,889 (1948)
3,558 (1947)   1946 Mercury Station Wagon

Red striping detail in the grille design of 1946 Fords set them apart from the later 1947-48 models, which had plain radiator grille bars. Other notable differences are the shape and location of the parking lamps, design of the hood ornament, width of the body and fender mouldings, and a large bright-metal nameplate on the rear deck lid of 1947-48 models which replaced the two chrome strips of 1946 models. The 1948 Ford models were simply a continuation of the 1947's with very minor refinements.

There were an astonishing twenty-seven different Ford and Mercury coupes and sedans offered in the 1946-48 series. This led to a great deal of buyer confusion and the poor sales performance of some types. Only 20 of the Ford Deluxe Sedans were built in 1947 and none for 1948. Likewise, only 34 Tudor Mercury Sedans were produced in 1947 and none in 1948.

163,370
74,954 (Dlx) **1946 Ford Super Dlx Tudor Sedan**

1947 Ford Super Dlx Fordor Sedan

116,744
20 (Dlx)
92,056 (1946 Super Deluxe)
9,246 (1946 Dlx)
71,358 (1948 Super Dlx)

1948 Ford Super Dlx Tudor Sedan

82,161
23,356 (Dlx)
136,126 (1947 Super Dlx)
44,523 (1947 Dlx)

43,281
40,280 (1946)
24,283 (1948) **1947 Mercury Town Sedan**

13,108
34 (1947) **1946 Mercury Tudor Sedan**

70,826 1946 Ford Super Deluxe Sedan Coupe

12,249
10,670 (Dlx) 1946 Ford Super Dlx 5-Window Coupe

44,828
80,830 (1947) 1948 Ford Super Deluxe Sedan Coupe

10,872
5,048 (1948) 1947 Ford Super Dlx 5-Window Coupe

New 1946 Ford Sedan Coupes aboard a truckaway unit

24,163
29,284 (1947) 1946 Mercury Sedan Coupe
16,476 (1948)

179

Its once immaculate tiled floor showing the rigors of wartime use, Henry Ford's famed Highland Park Plant showroom is pictured at the right serving as a facility leased to a local dealer. An entire range of Ford-Lincoln-Mercury new and customer cars can be observed.

Mediocre demand prompted the decision to drop the Sedan Delivery body type at the end of the 1947 Ford production run. It would reappear in 1952 as the Courier— an adaptation of the Ranch Wagon. Extremely low in numbers produced, the 1946-47 Ford Sedan Deliveries shared the same body shell with the 1942 model and had the usual 1946-47 trim differences. The driving and cargo compartments were fully lined; there was a wide rubber-sealed rear door; and objects up to 10½ feet long could be loaded inside past the driver's seat.

A view of the service department at Park Motor Sales

3,187
3,484 (1947)

1946 Ford Sedan Delivery

n Dearborn, Michigan, August 2, 1946

The first civilian post-War Ford Pickups were officially the 1945 "Commercial Cars"— facelifted 1942 models put into production to ease the domestic situation. In view of material shortages, the 1945-47 models had just the bare essentials with painted trim and scant brightwork. Rubber being in short supply, even the side mount spare tire was left off assembled units on through the production run which lasted until a new design Pickup was introduced in January, 1948 *(originally intended as part of the 1949 model line and pictured in the next chapter).*

75,088
62,072 (1947)

1946 Ford Pickup

1946 FORD STANDARDS AND OPTIONS

Engine: *90hp 6-cyl or 100hp V8*, Transmission: *3-speed manual*, Wheelbase: *114-inches*

CAR BODY COLORS

Black, Light Moonstone Gray, Navy Blue, Botsford Blue Green, Modern Blue, Dynamic Maroon, Dark Slate Gray Metallic, Willow Green

CONVERTIBLE COLORS

Black, Light Moonstone Gray, Navy Blue, Botsford Blue Green, Modern Blue, Dynamic Maroon, Dark Slate Gray Metallic

INSTRUMENT PANEL

Super Deluxe *Gun Metal Blue Metallic* with *Blue-Gray* plastic ornamentation, Deluxe *Light Tan Metallic* with *Dark Tan* plastic ornamentation, Late Club Convertible, Sportsman, and Station Wagon *Sequoia Grain (maplewood)*

UPHOLSTERY

	Tan, Red or Gray Genuine Leather	Tan, Red or Gray Artificial Leather & Bedfd. Cord	Tan Genuine Leather	Gray Stripe Broadcloth	Gray-Stripe Mohair	Tan Stripe Broadcloth	Tan Stripe Mohair
Super Deluxe Closed Cars	—	—	—	yes	yes	—	—
Deluxe Closed Cars	—	—	—	—	—	yes	yes
Sportsman	yes	—	—	—	—	—	—
Club Convt.	yes	yes	—	—	—	—	—
Station Wagon	—	—	yes	—	—	—	—

1946 MERCURY STANDARDS AND OPTIONS

Engine: *100hp V8*, Transmission: *3-speed manual*, Wheelbase: *118-inches*

COLORS

Light Moonstone Gray, Navy Blue, Botsford Blue-Green, Modern Blue, Dynamic Maroon, Greenfield Green, Dark Slate Gray Metallic, Silver Sand Metallic, Willow Green, Black

INSTRUMENT PANEL

Closed models optional *Brown Metallic* with *Gray Plastic* or *Gray-Green Metallic* with *Gray-Green Plastic*, Convertible *Metallic Maroon* (early) or *Walnut Wood Grain*, Sportsman and Station Wagon *Walnut Wood Grain*

UPHOLSTERY

	Mercury Rust Broadcloth	Gray-Green Bedford Cord	Tan Genuine Leather	Red Genuine Leather	Gray Genuine Leather
Closed Cars	yes	yes	—	—	—
Convertible & Station Wagon	—	—	yes	yes	yes

1946-48 GENUINE FORD AND MERCURY ACCESSORIES

Authorized accessories for most years include: Radio, Heater, Defroster, Seat Covers, Road Lamps, WSW Tires, Spotlight, Sideview Mirror, Cigar Lighter, Locking Gas Cap, License Plate Frames, Governor, Underseal, Back-up Lights, Windshield Wipers, Hand Brake Signal, Brake Booster, Tire & Fire Unit, Auto. Rear Door Locks, Grille Guard, Bumper End Guards, Gas Lid Lock, Portable Utility Light, Windshield Wiper Vacuum Tank, Foot Operated Tire Pump, Radio Foot Control, Electric Clock, Wheel Trim Rings, Fender Shields, Dynamatic Fan, Radiator Insect Screen, and Winterfront.

1947-48 FORD-MERCURY STANDARDS AND OPTIONS

Ford engine: *100hp V8 or 90hp 6-cyl,* Transmission: *3-speed manual,* Wheelbase: *114-inches*
Mercury engine: *100hp V8,* Transmission: *3-speed manual,* Wheelbase: *118-inches*

CAR BODY COLORS

Medium Luster Black, Rotunda Gray, Barcelona Blue, Monsoon Maroon, Glade Green, Feather Gray
★ *Blue Gray Metallic,* ★ ★ *Parrot Green Metallic, Tucson Tan,* ☆ *Maize Yellow,* ☆ *Pheasant Red,*
★ ★ *Taffy Tan,* ☆ ☆ *Strata Blue,* ☆ ☆ *Shoal Green Gray*
★ Ford only, ★ ★ Mercury only, ☆ Convt. only, ☆ ☆ 1948 models only

FORD INSTRUMENT PANEL

Super Deluxe and Deluxe models *Gun Metal Metallic,* with *Gray plastic*
Convertible, Sportsman and Station Wagon models *Maplewood Grain*

FORD UPHOLSTERY

	Tan or Red Pebble Grain Leather	Tan or Red Art. Leather & Bedford Cord	Tan Vinyl or Leather	Blue Broadcloth	Broadcloth	Mohair
Super Deluxe Closed Cars	—	—	—	yes	yes	yes
Deluxe Closed Cars	—	—	—	—	yes	yes
Club Convt.	—	yes	—	—	—	—
Sportsman	yes	—	—	—	—	—
Station Wagon	—	—	yes	—	—	—

MERCURY INSTRUMENT PANEL

Closed models *Silver Gray* with *Gray plastic,* Convertible and Station Wagon *Walnut wood-grain*

MERCURY UPHOLSTERY

	Tan or Red Bedford Cord & Genuine Leather	Tan Genuine Leather	Tan-Gray Cloth
Closed cars	—	—	yes
Convertible	yes	—	—
Station Wagon	—	yes	—

This 1947 Ford accessory display includes Heater, Bumper End Guards, and Chrome Fender Shields.

The revolutionary 1949 Ford models were first shown at a stunning exhibition staged in New York City.

Ford dealers and distinguished guests preview the splendid new 1949 models at the Waldorf Astoria Hotel June 8, 1948. In one bold move Henry Ford II had eclipsed the renowned showmanship of his famous grandfather by staging the most glamorous one-room auto show of all time. The toyland setting of color, action, and real models would captivate visitors throughout the week-long showing.

NINE

All-American 1949-51 Models

NEW York City's magnificent Waldorf-Astoria Hotel pulsed with excitement. It was June 10, 1948, and people swarmed through its elegant corridors and ballrooms to view the sensational new 1949 Ford line.

Swept along through the anterooms where the Lincolns and Mercurys were on glittering exhibit, the crowd found the supreme moment when it arrived in the gold-and-white satin trimmed Grand Ballroom. Here, in glorious splendor was perhaps the greatest automobile spectacle ever staged. On a revolving turntable rode five sparkling Fords which represented all of the new body types. As the cars slowly moved by, smiling models waved and mirrors at the center of the carousel flashed fragmented reflections of the cars in a dazzling display of optical illusion washed by a cascade of light from the overhead canopy.

Transfixed by this near-fantasy, the visitor had only to turn his head and be awed by the giant rotisserie that rose high off the floor to embrace a pair of full-size Ford cutaway chassis which rotated on an axis and at the same time exhibited their working parts in fully engaged motion.

This was Henry Ford II's show. Since the day he took over the ailing Ford Motor Company in September, 1945, his primary aim had been to restore the Company's leadership in the low-price car market, and this public introduction of cars bearing his own stamp was to be the kick-off. He had gambled $72 million on tooling for the new 1949 models and spent another $10 million for advertising. Now it was time to show his hand to the public.

He gave them a good idea of what to expect when he had unveiled his new Lincolns and Mercurys six weeks earlier . . . both cars had radical new styling with lower, wider, flowing body lines, more window area and a new chassis. It was the Mercury which first broke Ford medium and low-price car tradition by having coil springs up front and longitudinal springs at the rear— instead of the old "buggy-style" transverse springs.

Now, at the Waldorf, the public was seeing this same treatment on the Ford line. Together with sweeping changes in mechanical design and styling, the 1949 model presented a low silhouette with large glass area, sheer sides, and a daring grille design suggestive of a bullet in winged flight. From the front, top, side, and bottom views the cars were totally new from stem to stern. Only the flathead V8 engine remained from past history, and even it had been dressed up to look fashionable and function better.

It was an automobile promotion like no other in the history of Ford Motor Company since the introduction of the Model A. Buyers flocked to dealers' showrooms in the ensuing months, and sales rocketed to the highest levels since 1930. When the slightly modified and improved 1950 Ford and Mercury models were introduced in mid-November, 1949, sales took off again to top the record of Ford passenger car production set in 1929— and nearly top the 1925 figure. The pattern held in 1951 to make Henry Ford II's roll of the dice one of the biggest pay-offs for a 31 year-old in the annals of American business.

Perhaps it was the youth of their creator, but these low-slung, speedy 1949-51 Fords and Mercurys are today the very essence of "the fabulous fifties street machine."

Few Americans old enough to be interested in cars would fail to notice that Ford Motor Company had some new models to show in the summer of 1948. Introduced six months earlier than normal, the 1949 Fords received a spirited public reception behind a huge advertising campaign. In the photos opposite and below visitors to dealer showrooms in Louisville, Kentucky, size up the ''Forty-Niners.''

Looking over an enticing 1949 Ford Tudor Sedan

A prospect examines a 1949 Ford Coupe interior at a Louisville dealer showroom as visitors crowd the floor.

A Waldorf Astoria crowd ogles a 1949 Ford Convertible and the alluring driver

85,111
35,120 (Deluxe Bus)

1950 Ford Custom Deluxe Club Coupe

Classy as the 1949 models were, the 1950 Fords had just the right styling refinements to make them even more popular. This 1950 Club Coupe is high fashion motoring for the society matron of the era who wished to look sporty but did not want to be bothered with a convertible. The nifty back seat held three extra passengers with ample leg room.

Visitors to the 1950 Michigan State Fair get a Ford lecture.

150,254
4,170 (Dlx)   28,946 (Dlx Bus Cpe)
1949 Ford Custom Deluxe Club Coupe

20,343
53,263 (Cust Dlx)   1951 Ford Deluxe Business Coupe

Cutaway cars have been a tradition at auto shows from the very beginning, and Ford used them extensively with the V8. Here, at the Michigan State Fair September 5, 1950, a Ford man points out features of the new Fordor Sedan.

Coupes in the 1949-51 Ford series were the most handsomely proportioned of the body types in the line and came in either the 6-passenger Club variety or the single-seat Business model with a large parcel shelf behind the split seat. The Club Coupes had push-out, pivoting-type side windows in the rear; and notable features on cars with Custom equipment were wheels in body colors, and chrome trim around the windshield and back window.

Two-tone 1949 Mercury at a Los Angeles dealership   *Two-tone 1950 Mercury on exhibit at an auto show*

120,616   1949 Mercury 6-Passenger Coupe

151,489   1950 Mercury 6-Passenger Coupe

142,168   1951 Mercury 6-Passenger Coupe

Out for a drive in their new Mercury, a city couple asks a
farmer for directions. The 1949-51 Mercury Coupes were
easily the sportiest of their type on the market and were
highly esteemed by younger buyers. Longer rear fenders
and wider grille bars marked the 1951 Mercurys. Closed
models for all three years were available in two-tone paint
schemes— for the first time since 1941.

50,299   1950 Ford Custom Deluxe Convertible Club Coupe

40,934   1951 Ford Custom Deluxe Convertible Club Coupe

51,133   1949 Ford Custom Deluxe Convertible Club Coupe

Among America's best selling and most nostalgic convertibles were the 1949-51 Ford models. Beautiful to look at and delightful to drive these flashy cars turned heads at the country club as well as on the campus and popularized such colors as Chartreuse, Miami Cream, and Matador Red. These were the first sedan-type convertibles built by Ford since 1940 and met an enthusiastic reception in the marketplace as sales boomed 400 per cent over the previous convertible series. The colorful interior of the 1949 car came in a buyer's choice of Red, Tan, or Green leather combined with Bedford cord to harmonize with the body color. Buyers of the 1950 model had a choice of seven different interior combinations and 1951 buyers had their choice of eight.

CHRYSLER

STUDEBAKER

LINCOLN

44

The Ford Motor Company exhibit at the 1950 Motor Show at Geneva, Switzerland

195

As Henry Ford's son Edsel had shaped the design of the Company's pre-World War II cars, Edsel's son Benson shaped the Mercurys of the post-War period. At the right, the young head of Lincoln-Mercury Division sits at the wheel of a 1950 Mercury Convertible— the official pace car for that year's Indy "500". In the passenger seat is famed race car driver and track executive Wilbur Shaw. Benson's appealing 1949-51 Mercury Convertibles were targeted for upper middle class buyers who wanted a little more flair and comfort in their cars than that of their neighbor's Fords. The smooth lines and classy stance of his convertibles did that and more as they were destined to rank high among America's most admired "dream cars."

Benson Ford in the 1950 Indianapolis "500" pace car

8,341   1950 Mercury 6-Passenger Convertible Coupe

16,765   1949 Mercury 6-Passenger Convertible Coupe

6,759   1951 Mercury 6-Passenger Convertible Coupe

155,882   1949 Mercury Sport Sedan

From the rear perspective the 1949-50 Mercurys were close in appearance excepting that the 1949 model had a three-piece rear window. The hubcaps were also different— the 1949 cars were emblazoned with the lettering "Mercury Eight," while the 1950 cars had unadorned wheel covers. The 1951 Mercury received extensive restyling with rear fenders extending in a bold sweep to the rear of the car, wrap-around rear bumpers that blended into a chrome quarter panel trim, new combination taillight and directional signal, new deck lid handle and hub caps, and a large back window. A new option available on the 1951 Mercury was the "Merc-O-Matic" automatic transmission that had been developed jointly by Ford and Borg-Warner.

132,082   1950 Mercury Sport Sedan

157,648   1951 Mercury Sport Sedan

1949 Mercury Convertible interior

1951 Mercury Convertible interior

1950 Mercury Convertible interior

The 1949 Mercury instrument panel had a round clock-type speedometer with engine gauges set off with chrome bezels. For 1950-51 the panel was thoroughly restyled with the instruments nicely grouped to either side of a half-circle speedometer set below an "eyebrow" shade. Engine controls on the new models were positioned on an elaborate lower panel with the heater and vent knobs operated by moving them vertically in aviation-type slots.

1950 Ford closed car instrument panel

1951 Ford closed car instrument panel

Two special models introduced to the Ford line up in mid-1950 were the Mercury Monterey, which made its debut in June, and the Crestliner which appeared in July. The Monterey Coupe featured a grained vinyl-leather covering over the steel top and custom interior and exterior trim. It was available in three exterior color combinations, and the interior had chrome-plated garnish mouldings, two-tone instrument panel, special black steering wheel, and artificial leather headlining. The Crestliner was offered in Sportsman's Green with Black fabric top and Black airfoil side panels or in Coronation Red and Black. It came standard with fender skirts, twin side view mirrors, two-tone dash, special four-spoke steering wheel, and special interior decor.

While sales of the fabric-topped Monterey and Crestliner were disappointing, a car that would make a lasting impression was the new Victoria "hardtop convertible" model introduced with the 1951 Ford models. The first Ford closed car with a disappearing center door post, the Victoria got immediate notice from the young-at-heart who took to its sporty good looks.

110,286

1951 Ford Custom Victoria

200

1950 Mercury Monterey

1950 Ford Custom Crestliner

317,869
146,010 (Dlx)

1951 Ford Custom Deluxe Tudor Sedan

433,316
126,770 (Deluxe)

1949 Ford Custom Deluxe Tudor Sedan

398,060
275,360 (Deluxe)

1950 Ford Custom Deluxe Tudor Sedan

Easily the most popular in terms of price and style, the 1949-51 Custom Deluxe Tudors outsold all other Ford models by a wide margin. Narrow corner posts and body center pillars gave these models "picture window" visability and the "lounge car" interior was ample enough for three people to sit comfortably on each seat. The 1949 models had ribbed rubber front floor mats, while the 1950-51's had rubber with simulated carpet inserts. Rear mats in all three were genuine carpet. The 1949 Tudors could be ordered in Tan Vinyl upholstery throughout. In the photo above a Detroit businessman steps off a DC-3 to his waiting 1950 Tudor. In the photo on the opposite page a family enjoys a lakeside picnic and their new 1951 Tudor.

Conservative styling and easy passenger access gave the Fordor sedans a willing market among older families. Colors selected for 1949-51 models reflected that group's taste with nearly half of all Fordors ordered in shades of white or black. In the adjacent photo taken at the Somerville, Massachusetts, plant January 9, 1950, an inspector checks the paint on a car at the end of the infrared drying ovens. Since bodies and sheet metal parts were painted separately, color match was always critical, and it was found through experience that a variation of as little as 20 degrees in oven heat could result in an off color.

Inspecting a 1950 Fordor finish on the assembly line

247,181
77,888 (Deluxe)

1950 Ford Custom Deluxe Fordor Sedan

248,176
44,563 (Deluxe)

1949 Ford Custom Deluxe Fordor Sedan

232,691
54,265 (Deluxe)

1951 Ford Custom Deluxe Fordor Sedan

31,412

1949 Ford Custom Deluxe Station Wagon

With the revolutionary 1949 Fords came a totally new concept in building station wagons. The traditional "wood box" construction was supplanted by a low-profile all-steel body to which hardwood and plywood panels were bolted on strictly for decoration. The idea was to maintain the rugged good looks and tradition of the wood cars and yet eliminate the customary squeaks and groans by transferring body stresses to the two-door steel body shell. The complex bolt-on wood panels required bending at Iron Mountain by means of high-frequency radiation presses. Wood panel frames for the 1949-51 Ford models were in either Birch or Maple, with the plywood panels finished in grained Mahogany. Either or both of the rear seats lifted out of the 8-passenger cars. The 1949 model had a genuine leather front seat, while on the 1950 only the driver's portion was real leather. On the 1951 model the front seat was upholstered in tan vinyl. Passenger seats for all three years were covered in the vinyl material.

San Francisco dealers admire the new 1949 Ford Station Wagon

22,929   1950 Ford Custom Deluxe Station Wagon

29,017   1951 Ford Custom Deluxe Station Wagon

1,746   1950 Mercury Station Wagon

3,812   1951 Mercury Station Wagon

8,044

1949 Mercury Station Wagon

In its dual role as both a pleasure and business vehicle, the success of the station wagon has been attributed to its versatility. From hauling hay bales to kids, dogs, and bass fiddles, the cars were so handy that sales skyrocketed 400 per cent between 1940 and 1950. By that time Ford was producing 40 per cent of all the station wagons made in the world. However, its great Iron Mountain plant would soon be closed as the increased use of steel in the bodies and the need for increased production would require a new plant closer to Dearborn. In its final swan song, the great hardwood mill would produce the glamorous 1949-51 models— including these top-of-the-line Mercurys.

148,956
104,803 (1949)
108,006 (1948)

1950 Ford Pickup

117,414

1951 Ford Pickup

Of all the radically new Ford Motor Company vehicles intended for introduction as 1948 models, only the truck line appeared. This was in January, 1948— several months before the new (redesignated 1949) passenger cars made their debut. The Pickup followed the general truck design with dramatically changed body shape, flat-top "square" fenders, one-piece windshield, recessed grille, chrome and stainless steel ornamentation, and a spacious interior. A novel feature was the center bar in the left hood grille which served as the hood release. The 1948 Pickup design was continued for 1949-50 with very minor revisions to detail. The 1951 model, on the other hand, had reworked front sheetmetal with a powerful new grille design.

After two decades the flathead V8 engine, as Henry Ford designed it, had changed little. The color of the Ford block went through a permutation during the years (Green 1932-42, Blue 1946-48, Bronze 1949-53) and some of its functions had been improved, but it was still the same concept. Horsepower in the Ford type had been increased from 65 in 1932 to 100 in 1951— and in the Mercury, from 95 in 1939 to 112 in 1951.

1950 Ford V8 engine on the assembly line at Buffalo, New York

Ford accessory display at a 1950 auto show

1949-51 GENUINE FORD AND MERCURY ACCESSORIES

OPTIONAL (or standard) ON ALL CARS

Radio, Heater, Defroster, Seat Covers, Road Lamps, WSW Tires, Spot Light, Side View Mirror, Cigar Lighter, Locking Gas Cap, License Frames, Governor, Underseal, Back-up Lights, Windshield Washers, Non-glare Mirror, Rear Window Wiper, Exhaust Deflector, Grille Guard, Rear Seat Speakers, Wheel Trim Rings, Fender Shields.

FORD OPTIONS

Turn Indicators	*Door-top Side Mirror*	*Door-belt Side Mirror*
Rear Window Defroster	★ *Auto. Rear Door Locks*	*Bumper Guards*
Front Fender Guards	*Rocker Panel Trim*	★ *Gas Fill Signal*
Port. Utility Light	*Floor Mats*	*Windshield Visor*
Courtesy Lamp	*Glove Comp. Light*	*Window Vent Shades*
Star Fender Ornament	★★ *Custom Steering Wheel*	☆ *Full Hub Caps*
Hood Ornament	*Winterfront*	*Radiator Insect Screen*

★ 1949 item, ★★ 1950 item, ☆ 1951 item

MERCURY OPTIONS

Hand Brake Signal	☆ *Cowl Scuff Panels*	*Gas Lid Lock*
Curb Signal	★★ *Spare Air Assembly*	★★ *Luggage*
☆ *Ash Tray Light*	☆ *Foot Hassock*	★★ *Lap Robe*
★★ *Initial Plates*	★★ *Custom Steering Wheel*	*Spark Plug Protectors*
☆ *Underhood Insulation*		

★★ 1950 item, ☆ 1951 item

This list was taken directly from the Accessory Section of the Ford Body Parts Catalog. Parts easily interchanged between years but stars indicate model year the part was originally designated for. Many of the Ford items came standard on the Mercury.

211

1949 FORD STANDARDS AND OPTIONS

Engine: *100hp V8 or 95hp 6-cyl.*, Transmission: *3-speed manual*, Wheelbase: *114-inches*

CUSTOM AND FORD BODY COLORS

Black, Birch Gray, Midland Maroon Metallic, Sea-Mist Green, Meadow Green. Colony Blue

☆ CUSTOM MODELS ONLY

Bayview Blue Metallic, ★ *Gun Metal Gray Metallic*
☆ wheels to match body color   ★ not available on Station Wagon

CONVERTIBLE CLUB COUPE ONLY

Miami Cream, Fez Red

INSTRUMENT PANEL (except Convt.)

Silver Gray Metallic

CONVERTIBLE BODY COLOR AND UPHOLSTERY COMBINATIONS

BODY	UPHOLSTERY COLOR
Black	*Red, Tan, or Green*
Colony Blue	*Red or Tan*
Bayview Blue Metallic	*Tan*
Birch Gray	*Red, Tan, or Green*
Gun-Metal Gray Metallic	*Red*
Sea-Mist Green	*Tan or Red*
Midland Maroon Metallic	*Red or Tan*
Meadow Green	*Tan or Green*
Miami Cream	*Red, Tan, or Green*
Fez Red	*Red or Tan*

Convertible Coupes are upholstered with a combination of genuine leather and Bedford Cord. *Beige Bedford Cord* is used with either *Red or Tan Leather* and *Green Bedford Cord* is used in combination with *Green leather*.

Top material is *Gray-Tan, Black, or Green* to harmonize with the upholstery color scheme.

Instrument panel and interior metal is finished in colors to harmonize with genuine leather. *Red leather* interior metal color is *Midland Maroon Metallic*. With *Tan leather* metal color is *Tan Metallic*, and *Green leather* metal color is *Meadow Green*.

UPHOLSTERY

	Blue-Gray Tweed Broadcloth	Gray-Green Striped Mohair	Green-Stripe Broadcloth	Green & Red Stripe Broadcloth	Tan Genuine Leather	Tan Vinyl Leather
Custom Sedans & Club Coupe	*yes*	*yes*	—	—	—	—
Ford Sedans and Coupes	—	—	*yes*	*yes*	—	—
Station Wagon Driver's Seat	—	—	—	—	*yes*	—
Station Wagon Passenger Seats	—	—	—	—	—	*yes*
Optional on all Custom & Ford Sedans & Coupes	—	—	—	—	—	*yes*

1949 MERCURY STANDARDS AND OPTIONS

Engine: *110hp V8*, Transmission: *3-speed manual*, Wheelbase: *118-inches*

COLORS

Black, ☆*Alberta Blue, Royal Bronze Maroon Metallic, Dakota Gray,* ☆*Biscay Blue Metallic, Berwick Green Metallic, Bermuda Cream, Lima Tan Metallic, Tampico Red Metallic*
☆ not available on Convertible

TWO-TONE COLORS
(Sport Sedan and 6-pass. Coupe)

UPPER BODY	LOWER BODY
Banff Green Metallic	*Berwick Green Metallic*
Lima Tan Metallic	*Haiti Beige Metallic*

TOWN SEDAN, SPORT SEDAN AND SIX-PASSENGER COUPE UPHOLSTERY

Body Color	Green Check Broadcloth	Beige Cord	Blue Stripe Broadcloth
Black	yes	yes	yes
Alberta Blue	—	yes	yes
Royal Bronze Blue Met.	—	yes	yes
Dakota Gray	yes	—	yes
Biscay Blue Metallic	—	—	yes
Berwick Green Metallic	—	yes	yes
Bermuda Cream	yes	—	yes
Lima Tan Metallic	—	—	yes
Tampico Red Metallic	—	yes	—
Two-tone Green	yes	—	—
Two-tone Tan-Beige	—	yes	yes

CONVERTIBLE UPHOLSTERY

Body Color	Red or Tan Leather and Tan Cord		Green Leather and Green Cord
Black	yes	yes	yes
Royal Bronze Metallic	—	yes	—
Dakota Gray	yes	yes	yes
Berwick Green Met.	—	—	yes
Bermuda Cream	yes	yes	yes
Tampico Red Metallic	yes	yes	—

Top material is *Black* with *Black* binding, *Black* with *Red* binding, *Gray-Tan* with *Gray-Tan* binding, or *Green* with *Green* binding to harmonize.

STATION WAGON

Tan Genuine Leather available in Wagon with all solid passenger car colors. *Red Genuine Leather* available with all colors but only *Tampico Red* of metallics. *Green Genuine Leather* available with *Black, Dakota Gray, Berwick Green Metallic,* and *Bermuda Cream* only.

1950 FORD STANDARDS AND OPTIONS

Engine: *100hp V8 or 95hp 6-cylinder*, Transmission: *3-speed Manual or optional Overdrive*, Wheelbase: *114-inches*

BODY COLORS (except Crestliner)

Sheridan Blue, Palisade Green, Dover Gray, Sunland Beige, Cambridge Maroon Metallic, Black

ADDITIONAL COLORS FOR CUSTOM DELUXE

Bimini Blue Metallic, Osage Green Metallic, Hawthorne Green Metallic

ADDITIONAL COLORS FOR CONVERTIBLE CLUB COUPE

Matador Red Metallic, Sportsman's Green

CRESTLINER COLOR SCHEMES

The two available exterior colors are *Sportsman's Green* with *Black* top and *Black* airfoil or *Coronation Red* with *Black* top and *Black* side panels. Interior options are combination *Black Leather* and harmonizing pin-striped *Bedford Cord* to match exterior color. Instrument panel is two-tone with body color upper and satin-finish *Black* lower.

INSTRUMENT PANEL

Deluxe Sedans and Business Coupe *Light Gray Metallic* or *Tan Metallic* Custom Deluxe Sedans and Club Coupe *Light Gray Metallic*. Convertible metal interior areas are painted *Sportsman's Green* with all combinations using *Chartreuse* leather, *Matador Red Metallic* with *Red* leather, and *Tan Metallic* with *Tan* leather. Station Wagon panel is *Mahogany* grain.

CLOSED CAR UPHOLSTERY

	Gray & Rust Stripe Mohair	Blue & Rust Stripes on Tan Broadcloth	Gray & Red Stripes on Gray Mohair	Gray & Blue Stripes on Gray Broadcloth
Deluxe Sedans and Business Coupe	*yes*	*yes*	—	—
Custom Deluxe Sedans and Club Coupe	—	—	*yes*	*yes*

STATION WAGON UPHOLSTERY

Station Wagon is upholstered in combination genuine leather, artificial leather and vinyl in *Tan shades.*

CONVERTIBLE CLUB COUPE COLOR COMBINATIONS

UPHOLSTERY	BODY COLOR
Light Tan Leather	*Sportsman's Green, Sunland Beige, Palisade Green, Hawthorne Green Metallic, Osage Green Metallic, Bimini Blue Metallic, Cambridge Maroon Metallic, Sheridan Blue, Black*
Two-tone Tan Leather or Two-tone Tan Leather and Tan Bedford Cord	*Sunland Beige, Palisade Green, Hawthorne Green Metallic, Osage Green Metallic, Cambridge Maroon Metallic, Sheridan Blue, Black*
Chartreuse & Black all leather or combination Bedford Cord	*Sportsman's Green, Black*
Red & Black all leather or combination Bedford Cord	*Matador Red Metallic, Dover Gray, Sunland Beige, Osage Green Metallic, Bimini Blue Metallic, Sheridan Blue, Black*

Convertible top material is *Black, Tan,* or *Green* to harmonize

1950 MERCURY STANDARDS AND OPTIONS

Engine: *110hp V8*, Transmission: *3-speed manual with optional Overdrive*, Wheelbase: *118-inches*

CLOSED CAR SCHEMES (except Monterey)

UPHOLSTERY	BODY COLOR
Two-tone Tan and Bedford Cord	Black, Royal Bronze Maroon, Trojan Gray, Everglade Green, Dune Beige, Roanoke Green Metallic, Maywood Green Metallic
Gray Block	Black, Royal Bronze Maroon, Trojan Gray, Banning Blue Metallic, Laguna Blue Metallic
Blue-gray Two-tone plain	Banning Blue Metallic, Laguna Blue Metallic, Black, Royal Bronze Maroon, Trojan Gray
Blue-gray Nylon Cord	Black, Royal Bronze Maroon, Trojan Gray, Banning Blue Metallic, Laguna Blue Metallic

MONTEREY COLOR SCHEMES

The Monterey is available in three exterior color combinations: *Black* with *Yellow* landau-grain vinyl top; *Cortaro Red Metallic* with *Black* top; and *Turquoise Blue* with *Dark Blue* top. Upholstery options are harmonizing shades of genuine leather or combinations of leather and Bedford Cord.

CONVERTIBLE COLOR SCHEMES

Red and Black Leather	Black, Trojan Gray, Dune Beige, Mirada Yellow
Light and Dark Blue Leather	Black, Royal Bronze Maroon, Trojan Gray, Banning Blue Metallic, Laguna Blue Metallic, Mirada Yellow
Light and Dark Blue Leather and Gray Nylon	Black, Royal Bronze Maroon, Trojan Gray, Banning Blue Metallic, Laguna Blue Metallic, Mirada Yellow
Two-tone Tan all Leather	Black, Royal Bronze Maroon, Trojan Gray, Everglade Green, Dune Beige, Roanoke Green Metallic, Maywood Green Metallic, Mirada Yellow

Convertible top material is *Black* with *Black* binding, *Black* with *Red* binding,
Tan with *Tan* binding, or *Green* with *Green* binding to harmonize.

STATION WAGON COLOR SCHEMES

Tan Leather	Black, Royal Bronze Maroon, Trojan Gray, Everglade Green, Banning Blue Metallic, Dune Beige, Laguna Blue Metallic, Roanoke Green Metallic, Maywood Green Metallic
Green Leather	Black, Trojan Gray, Everglade Green, Dune Beige, Roanoke Green Metallic, Maywood Green Metallic
Red Leather	Black, Royal Bronze Maroon, Trojan Gray, Banning Blue Metallic, Dune Beige, Laguna Blue Metallic

CLOSED CAR TWO-TONE COLOR COMBINATIONS (Except Monterey)

UPHOLSTERY	UPPER	LOWER
Two-tone Tan and Bedford Cord	Penrod Tan	Dune Beige
	Trojan Gray	Roanoke Green
	Roanoke Green	Trojan Gray
Gray Block or Blue-Gray Two-tone plain or Blue-gray Nylon Cord	Trojan Gray	Banning Blue
	Banning Blue	Trojan Gray
	Trojan Gray	Laguna Blue
	Laguna Blue	Trojan Gray

1951 MERCURY STANDARDS AND OPTIONS

Engine: *112hp V8*, Transmission *3-speed manual or optional Merc-O-Matic or Overdrive*, Wheelbase: *118-inches*

SPORT SEDAN AND 6-PASSENGER COUPE COLOR SCHEMES

Body Color	Tan & Gray Stripe Broadcloth	Two-tone Tan Pinstripe Broadcloth	Gray Block Broadcloth	Blue Stripe Nylon Cord	Two-tone Green Stripe Broadcloth	Tan Leather
Black	yes	yes	yes	yes	yes	yes
Banning Blue Metallic	—	—	yes	yes	—	yes
Everglade Green	yes	yes	—	—	yes	yes
Luxor Maroon Metallic	yes	yes	yes	yes	—	yes
Kerry Blue Metallic	—	—	yes	yes	—	yes
Mission Gray	yes	—	yes	yes	yes	yes
Coventry Green Gray	yes	yes	—	—	yes	yes
Sheffield Green	yes	yes	—	—	yes	yes
Tomah Ivory	yes	yes	yes	yes	yes	yes

MONTEREY COLOR SCHEMES

UPHOLSTERY

Seal Brown Leather with
Seal Brown and Turquoise Cord

Oyster White and Medium Green all Leather

Red and Black all Leather

BODY COLOR

Turqoise with
Seal Brown top

Brewster Green Metallic with Oyster White top

Monterey Red Metallic with Black top

CONVERTIBLE AND STATION WAGON COLOR SCHEMES

Body Color	Red & Black Leather	Brown Golden Tan Leather	Blue & Ivory Leather	Blue Leather & Nylon Cord	Two-tone Red Vinyl	Tan & Chestnut Brown Vinyl	Two-tone Green Vinyl
Black	yes	yes	yes	yes	yes	yes	yes
Banning Blue Metallic	yes	—	yes	yes	yes	yes	—
Everglade Green	—	Yes	—	—	—	yes	yes
Luxor Maroon Metallic	yes	yes	yes	yes	yes	yes	—
Kerry Blue Metallic	yes	—	yes	yes	yes	yes	—
Mission Gray	yes	—	yes	yes	yes	yes	yes
Coventry Green Gray	—	yes	—	—	yes	yes	yes
Sheffield Green	—	yes	—	—	—	yes	yes
Tomah Ivory	yes	yes	yes	yes	yes	yes	yes
Vassar Yellow (convt. only)	yes	yes	yes	yes	—	—	—

Convertible top material is *Black, Black* with *Red* binding, *Gray-Tan*, or *Green* to harmonize.

SPORT SEDAN AND 6-PASSENGER COUPE TWO-TONE COMBINATIONS

UPHOLSTERY	UPPER	LOWER
Tan and Gray Stripe Broadcloth or Two-tone Tan Pinstripe Broadcloth	Black	Tomah Ivory
	Tomah Ivory	Sheffield Green
	Sheffield Green	Tomah Ivory
	Sheffield Green	Coventry Green Gray
	Coventry Green Gray	Sheffield Green
Two-tone Green Stripe Broadcloth	Coventry Green Gray	Everglade Green
	Everglade Green	Coventry Green Gray
Gray Block Broadcloth or Blue Stripe Nylon Cord	Black	Tomah Ivory
	Mission Gray	Banning Blue Metallic
	Banning Blue Metallic	Mission Gray

1951 FORD STANDARDS AND OPTIONS

Engine: *100hp V8 or 95hp 6-cyl.*, Transmission: *3-speed Manual with optional Overdrive or Fordamatic*, Wheelbase: *114-inches*

BODY COLORS (Except Crestliner)

Sheridan Blue, Alpine Blue, Raven Black, Sea Island Green, Silvertone Gray, Mexacalli Maroon Metallic, ★ *Hawthorne Green Metallic,* ★ *Greenbrier Metallic,* ★ *Culver Blue Metallic,* ★ *Hawaiian Bronze Metallic,* ☆ *Sportsman's Green.*
★ color for Custom models and Station Wagons, ☆ color for Convertible Coupe

CRESTLINER COLOR SCHEMES

UPHOLSTERY	BODY, HOOD, FENDERS	TOP, SIDE, AND REAR SECTION
Black artificial leather &	*Greenbrier Metallic*	*Black*
Chartreuse or Blue-Green	*Sportsman's Green*	*Black*
Craftcord or Brown artificial	*Hawaiian Bronze Metallic*	*Brown*
leather with Tan Craftcord	*Light Tan*	*Black*

INSTRUMENT PANEL

Deluxe Sedans and Business Coupe *Satin Silver* and *Gray Metallic*, Crestliner, Club Coupe, and Custom Sedans in colors to harmonize with upholstery, Station Wagon *Dark Reddish Brown* upper and *Dark Prima Vera grain* lower.

Convertible instrument panel's major metal surfaces are painted *Blue Green Metallic* with combinations using *Blue Green* leather, *Red Metallic* with *Red* leather, *Sportsman's Green* with *Chartreuse* leather, and *Tan Metallic* with *Tan* leather.

CUSTOM SEDANS AND CLUB COUPE UPHOLSTERY

UPHOLSTERY AND INTERIOR FINISH	BODY COLOR
Tan and Rust Stripe Craftloom *Brown Metallic paint*	*any closed car color*
Gray Stardot Craftweave *Blue Gray Metallic paint*	*Raven Black, Sheridan Blue, Alpine Blue, Culver Blue Metallic, Silvertone Gray*
Green Starcheck Craftweave *Green Metallic paint*	*Hawthorne Green Metallic, Greenbrier Metallic, Sea Island Green*
Two-tone Brown Craftcord *Brown Metallic paint*	*Mexacalli Maroon Metallic, Hawaiian Bronze Metallic*

CONVERTIBLE CLUB COUPE COLOR COMBINATIONS

UPHOLSTERY	BODY COLOR
Two-tone Tan leather or two-tone Tan leather and Tan Craftcord	*Raven Black, Sheridan Blue, Culver Blue Metallic, Alpine Blue, Mexacalli Maroon Metallic, Hawaiian Bronze Metallic, Hawthorne Green Metallic, Greenbrier Metallic, Sea Island Green*
Chartreuse and Black leather or Chartreuse and Black & Chartreuse Craftcord	*Raven Black, Sportsman's Green*
Red & Black leather or Red & Black leather & Red Craftcord	*Raven Black, Sheridan Blue, Culver Blue Metallic, Sea Island Green, Silvertone Gray, Mexacalli Maroon Metallic*
Blue-Green and Black leather Blue-Green and Black leather and Blue-Green Craftcord	*Raven Black, Silvertone Gray, Greenbrier Metallic, Sea Island Green*

Convt. top material is *Black, Black* with *Red* binding, *Gray-Tan* or *Green* to harmonize with body color

Ordered to Korean waters, a sailor bids adieu to his sweetheart and the new '52.

TEN

Last of the Flathead Fords

THERE was a war raging in Korea that tested the American will and resources but it didn't alter the excitement of another introduction of a totally restyled series of Ford and Mercurys.

"Ford dealers throughout the United States report that their showrooms are still crowded with people inspecting the new 1952 Ford cars and trucks which made their debut February 1st," reported an auto column. "The public has expressed keen interest in the curved windshield and rear window of the completely new design. The innovative suspended power pivot clutch and brake pedals, and the center gas filler location is getting a lot of attention. Women visitors seem to be favorably impressed with the wide choice of body colors and harmonizing interior trim while the men are more attracted to the new "Mileage Maker Six" and "Strato-Star V8" engines.

Similar praise was given the new Mercury for its swept-forward body lines that were accented with ornamentation suggestive of birds and planes in flight. It had more horsepower than the 1951 model, more color and upholstery options, and yet retailed for nearly the same price.

But it wasn't until the debut of the more refined and sophisticated 1953 models late in the year that interest in the new series really caught fire. Preceded by the announcement that Ford was planning a big celebration in the coming months to observe its 50th anniversary, the 1953 Ford line went on display at 6,400 dealerships across the country Friday, December 12, 1953.

Coincidentally, this would also be the last hurrah for the respected flathead Ford V8 engine which had given such lasting service and had proven Henry Ford's idea so right. Ensuing Ford and Mercury models would have the totally reengineered overhead valve V8 engines.

Featuring a highly-touted "Miracle Ride" suspension, the 1953 Fords were given a longer look with the addition of a moulding strip along the rear fenderline and new "jet-tube" tail lights. Grille and parking lights had been modified and other refinements included a new deck lid handle mounted below the Ford crest, with a concealed spring-loaded key opening.

It would be a memorable year for Ford Motor Company. In April, a pictorial book *Ford at Fifty* was published and distributed to employees and the public; Norman Rockwell was commissioned to create six illustrations for a commemorative calendar; Pulitzer prize historian Allan Nevins was asked to write a three volume history of the Company; the Ford Archives was dedicated in May; and a 1953 Ford Convertible was designated to pace the Indianapolis "500" mile starting lineup.

Then in June, President Eisenhower arrived in Dearborn for the dedication of the new Ford Research and Engineering Center; a specially prepared company history film "The American Road" was released; the Rotunda showplace was reopened to the public for the first time since 1942; Ed Sullivan dedicated his June 14 show to his sponsor's anniversary; and on the eve of the Company's birthday the following night one of the most memorable two-hour TV specials of all time was aired.

Carried on both CBS and NBC channels during prime time, the Leyland Hayward production featured a narration by Edward R. Murrow and Oscar Hammerstein II with performances by Rudy Vallee, Judith Anderson, Ethel Merman, and Mary Martin. The $500,000 extravaganza was a romp through the history of America over the previous 50 years and brought glowing reviews and thousands of new Ford admirers.

The entire year was a jubilee celebration of Ford Motor Company's contribution to the American scene over the past half-century. It was also the turning point for new concepts in Ford cars that would no longer require a flathead V8 engine.

A suburban couple decide on a new 1952 Ford Convertible.

Presented nearly three months late because of Korean War restrictions and an all-new body change, the 1952 Ford and Mercury line was nevertheless well received. In the scene above, a young couple looks over the colorful and spacious interior of their selection at Stuart Wilson Ford in Dearborn, Michigan.

Ready to write it up, a Texas dealer works with a couple interested in a snazzy 1952 Ford Convertible.

Dealers previewing the new 1952 Mercurys, give the Monterey Convertible high marks.

Designated the "Sunliner" model in the Crestliner series, the Ford convertible for 1952-53 came in a variety of body colors and upholstery options. Both Ford and Mercury convertibles for these years are noted for their bright tops which were available in four individual colors to harmonize with the body and upholstery scheme. The Ford top boot was made of vinyl in the same shade as the dark portion of the upholstery, with the binding in the same shade as the lighter portion of the upholstery.

40,861   1953 Ford Crestline Sunliner Convertible

8,463   1953 Mercury Monterey Convertible

22,534   1952 Ford Crestline Sunliner Convertible

5,261   1952 Mercury Monterey Convertible

223

Backed by banners on the walls offering strong opinions, a West Texas dealer dickers with a prospect over a new 1952 Ford Sedan. In the lower photo a 1953 Sedan is shown on sale at a Louisville, Kentucky, dealership. Displayed in the foreground is a sporty Ford V8 convertible. The Tudor Sedan at the auto show pictured at the right has the accessory grille guard, full hubcaps, rocker panel trim, window shades, fender skirts, door top mirror, white sidewall tires, and optional two-tone paint scheme to demonstrate how these cars could be dolled up.

175,762
79,931 (Mainline)
188,303 (Cust. Fordor)
41,277 (Main. Fordor)

1952 Customline Tudor Sedan

374,487
305,433 (Tudor)

1953 Ford Customline Fordor Sedan

The Ford exhibit at the 1952 Chicago Auto Show

69,463
152,995 (Tudor)

1953 Ford Mainline Fordor Sedan

50,183   1953 Mercury 2-Door Sedan

25,812
83,475 (4-Dr)   1952 Mercury 2-Door Sedan

59,794

1953 Mercury 4-Door Sedan

Mercury Sedans for 1952-53 were very similar in appearance and were even offered at the same $2390 base price. Both the 2-door and 4-door models came standard with arm rests on all doors, coat hooks, and a robe cord. Optional equipment included green-tinted window glass, electric window lifts and seat adjustment, and Merc-O-Matic Drive or Touch-O-Matic Overdrive. Rear fender skirts and full disc hubcaps were also optional at extra cost.

26,550
43,990 (1953)

1952 Ford Club Coupe

Business Coupe and Club Coupe models were offered in the 1952-53 Ford line. The latter came only in the Customline series and had the traditional split front seats and assist straps to permit easy passenger entry to the rear seat.

A pretty driver models the driving compartment of a 1953 Ford sedan.

76,119
39,547 (Sport Cpe)

1953 Mercury Monterey Coupe

30,599
24,453 (Monterey)

1952 Mercury Sport Coupe

The 1952-53 Mercury Coupes could be ordered plain or fancy as these two photos attest. The car above has optional white sidewall tires, fender skirts, full hubcaps, two-tone paint, and rocker panel trim, while the car at the left has the equipment which came standard. Both models were upholstered in combinations limited to this body style. The 1952's had three choices of standard interior schemes and four which could be ordered at extra cost. There were no standard schemes available to the buyer of the 1953 Monterey Coupe. Instead, there was the choice of five interiors coordinated with a multitude of solid body colors or two-tones.

77,320

1952 Ford Victoria

128,302

1953 Ford Victoria

One of the most successful body types ever offered by Ford, the "hardtop" Victoria was the perfect answer for the sport who didn't have the weather or the desire for a convertible. The 1952-53 models had built in rear arm rests with ash trays, special upholstery trim, and came standard in a choice of 14 two-tone body color combinations.

10,575
6,225 (1952)

1953 Ford Courier

A sedan delivery type returned to the Ford line for the first time in five years with introduction of the Courier— a version of the new two-door Ranch Wagon. It was trimmed the same as the Mainline cars with a brown vinyl front seat, two-tone gray headlining and gray masonite inside body panelling.

Ford Pickup styling remained static for 1952 with very minor cosmetic changes to the hood trim. The big change came in 1953 when the completely new F-100 made its appearance. Characterized by a massive front-end overhang and recessed grille, these models pioneered a running series of F-100's that would become very popular. The 1953 model came standard or deluxe— the deluxe model having extra bright trim and chrome-plated grille "teeth". A standard model is shown below coming off the assembly line.

81,537

1952 Ford Pickup

116,437

1953 Ford Pickup

11,001

1953 Ford Country Squire

As the boom in station wagon popularity soared, Ford built the industry's first plant constructed exclusively for the building of these vehicles. The Wayne, Michigan, plant built the bodies and shipped them to other assembly plants, such as nearby Dearborn, where a Country Squire is shown in the photo above, being lowered to a chassis. In step with the new plant was the radical change in the way the new 4-door Ford-Mercury Station Wagons would be fabricated. Now the body side panels were part of the all-steel body and would have simulated Mahogany wood grain paper decals. Still, the framing around these panels was in genuine bolt-on Maple hardwood. Simulated Maple wood grains decals were also applied over the steel between the body belt lines and roof drip rail.

The 1952-53 Ford Ranch Wagons were plainer two-door models.

232

5,426

1952 Ford Country Squire

2,487
7,719 (1953)

1952 Mercury Station Wagon

1952 FORD STANDARDS AND OPTIONS

Engine: *110hp V8 or 101hp 6-cyl*, Transmission: *3-speed manual with optional Overdrive or Fordamatic*, Wheelbase: *115-inches*

SINGLE-TONE BODY COLORS

Raven Black, Woodsmoke Gray, Sheridan Blue, Alpine Blue, Shannon Green Metallic, Meadowbrook Green, Glen Mist Green, Hawaiian Bronze, Sandpiper Tan, Carnival Red Metallic, Sungate Ivory, Coral Flame Red

TWO-TONE BODY COLORS

BODY	TOP
Alpine Blue	*Sungate Ivory*
Carnival Red Metallic	*Sandpiper Tan*
Sungate Ivory	*Hawaiian Bronze*
Shannon Green Metallic	*Glen Mist Green*
Meadowbrook Green	*Sungate Ivory*
Raven Black	*Sungate Ivory*
Alpine Blue	*Sheridan Blue*
Hawaiian Bronze	*Sandpiper Tan*
Shannon Green Metallic	*Sandpiper Tan*
Sandpiper Tan	*Hawaiian Bronze*

INSTRUMENT PANEL

All models have interior metal to harmonize with upholstery in *Medium Gray Metallic, Dark Brown Metallic, Green Metallic, Goldtone Metallic, Dark Blue Metallic,* or *Raven Black*

UPHOLSTERY

	Tan Check Craftweave	Gray with Red Stripe Craftloom	Blue & Ivory Saddletex	Mahogany & Ivory Saddletex	Golden Tan & Mahogany Vinyl
Mainline	yes	yes	yes	yes	—
Ranch Wagon	—	—	—	—	yes

	Gray with Red Stripe Craftweave	Green Stripe Craftweave	Two-tone Tan Craftcord	Blue & Ivory Saddletex	Mahogany & Ivory Saddletex	Mahogany & Milan Straw Vinyl
Customline	yes	yes	yes	yes	yes	—
Country Sedan	—	—	—	—	—	yes

	Tan/Brown Stripe & Mahogany Vinyl	Gray/Blue Stripe Blue Vinyl	Gray Green Stripe Green Vinyl	Red Leather & Black Vinyl	Tan Leather & Mahogany Vinyl	Ivory Leather & Green Vinyl	Light Blue Leather Dark Blue Vinyl	Mahogany & Milan Straw Vinyl
Victoria	yes	yes	yes	—	—	—	—	—
Convertible	—	—	—	yes	yes	yes	yes	—
Country Squire	—	—	—	—	—	—	—	yes

CONVERTIBLE TOP

Top material is *Black* with *Black* binding, *Black* with *Red* binding, *Gray-Tan* with *Gray-Tan* binding or *Green* with *Dark Green* binding to harmonize with body color.

1952 MERCURY STANDARDS AND OPTIONS

Engine: *125 hp V8*, Transmission: *3-speed manual or optional Merc-O-Matic or Overdrive*, Wheelbase: *118-inches*

CLOSED CAR COMBINATIONS (except ☆ Monterey Coupe)

Body Color	Brown & White Brdcloth	Gray Broken Stripe Brdcloth	Green Broken Stripe Brdcloth	Green & Ivory Vinyl	Golden Tan & Chestnut Brown Vinyl	Ivory Vinyl & Green Nylon	Two-tone Brown Stripe Nylon	Two-tone Blue Stripe Nylon
Raven Black	yes	yes	yes	yes	yes	yes	yes	yes
Admiral Blue	—	yes	—	—	yes	—	yes	yes
Fanfare Maroon	yes	yes	—	—	yes	—	yes	—
Newport Gray	yes	yes	yes	yes	yes	yes	yes	yes
Lucern Blue	—	yes	—	—	yes	—	yes	yes
Pebble Tan	yes	—	—	—	yes	yes	yes	—
Academy Blue	—	yes	—	—	yes	—	—	yes
Hillcrest Green	yes	—	yes	yes	—	yes	yes	—
Coventry Green Gray	yes	—	yes	yes	—	yes	yes	—
Lakewood Green	—	—	yes	yes	—	yes	—	—
Vassar Yellow	—	—	—	—	—	yes	—	—

☆ Monterey Coupe in above colors and seven distinct upholstery combinations

CONVERTIBLE AND STATION WAGON COLOR COMBINATIONS

Body Color	Black & Cherry Red Vinyl	Green & Ivory Vinyl	Blue & Ivory Vinyl	Bittersweet & Ivory Vinyl	Red Vinyl & Tan Ivory Plastic	Green Vinyl & Tan Ivory Plastic
Raven Black	yes	yes	yes	yes	yes	yes
Admiral Blue	yes	—	yes	—	—	—
Fanfare Maroon	yes	—	yes	—	yes	—
Newport Gray	yes	yes	yes	—	—	—
Lucern Blue	yes	—	yes	—	yes	—
Pebble Tan	yes	yes	yes	yes	yes	yes
Academy Blue	yes	—	yes	—	—	—
Hillcrest Green	—	yes	—	—	—	yes
Coventry Green Gray	—	yes	—	—	—	—
Lakewood Green	—	yes	—	—	—	—
Vassar Yellow	yes	yes	yes	—	—	—

Convertible top material is *Black* with *Black* binding, *Black* with *Red* binding, *Gray-Tan* with *Tan* binding, and *Green* with *Green* binding

CLOSED CAR TWO-TONE COLOR COMBINATIONS

UPPER (or reverse)	LOWER	UPPER (no reverse)	LOWER
Raven Black	Pebble Tan	Lucern Blue	Admiral Blue
Raven Black	Lucern Blue	Hillcrest Green	Coventry Green Gray
Raven Black	Lakewood Green	Lakewood Green	Coventry Green Gray
Raven Black	Fanfare Maroon	Raven Black	Newport Gray
Raven Black	Coventry Green Gray	Pebble Tan	Fanfare Maroon
		Raven Black	Vassar Yellow

*Fifteen color combinations
of broadcloths and vinyls
to harmonize*

1953 FORD STANDARDS AND OPTIONS

Engine: *110hp V8 or 101hp 6-cyl*, Transmission: *3-speed manual*, Wheelbase: *115-inches*

SINGLE-TONE BODY COLORS

Raven Black, Woodsmoke Gray, Sheridan Blue, Glacier Blue, Timberline Green, Fern Mist Green, Seafoam Green, Polynesian Bronze, Sandpiper Tan, Carnival Red, ☆*Sungate Ivory,* and ★*Coral Flame Red*
☆Victoria and Sunliner Convertible only, ★Sunliner Convertible only

SUNGATE IVORY TWO-TONE COMBINATIONS

Combination Sungate Ivory top with following lower body color:
Glacier Blue, Fern Mist Green, Raven Black, ☆☆*Flamingo Red, Carnival Red,* and *Sheridan Blue*
☆☆Victoria combination only

OTHER TWO-TONE COMBINATIONS

BODY	TOP
Carnival Red	*Sandpiper Tan*
Glacier Blue	*Sheridan Blue*
Sandpiper Tan	*Polynesian Bronze*
Sungate Ivory	*Fern Mist Green*
Sungate Ivory	*Sheridan Blue*
Sungate Ivory	*Carnival Red*
Seafoam Green	*Timberline Green*
Polynesian Bronze	*Sandpiper Tan*

INSTRUMENT PANEL

Instrument panel, garnish mouldings and seat side shields are *Light Gray, Dark Green, Dark Blue, Raven Black* or *Goldtone,* color-keyed to match specific colors.

UPHOLSTERY

	Gray & Gold Stripe Craftcord	Blue & Ivory Vinyl	Mahog. & Ivory Vinyl	Two-Tone Tan Check	Green & White Diag.	Two-Tone Gray Stripe	Blue & Ivory Vinyl	Mahog. & Ivory Vinyl
Mainline Sedans and Coupes	*yes*	*yes*	*yes*	—	—	—	—	—
Customline Sedans & Coupes	—	—	—	*yes*	*yes*	*yes*	*yes*	*yes*

	Mahog. Vinyl & Brown Nylon	Blue Vinyl & Blue Nylon	Green Vinyl & Green Nylon	Black Leather & Red Vinyl	Brown, Green or Blue Leather & Ivory Vinyl
Crestline Victoria	*yes*	*yes*	*yes*	—	—
Sunliner Convt.	—	—	—	*yes*	*yes*

All of the above selections color-keyed to specific body colors. Convertible top material is *Black* with *Black* binding, *Black* with *Red* binding, *Gray-Tan* with *Gray-Tan* binding, and *Green* with *Dark Green* binding to harmonize.

1953 MERCURY STANDARDS AND OPTIONS

Engine: *125hp V8*, Transmission: *3-speed Manual*, or optional
Merc-O-Matic or *Overdrive*, Wheelbase: *118-inches*

CLOSED CAR COLOR COMBINATIONS (except ★Monterey Coupe)

Body Color	Gray & White Check	Brown & White Check	Green & White Check	Dk Gray & White Herring-bone Weave	Dk Green & White Herring-bone Weave	Light Blue Basket Weave	Light Brown Basket Weave	Ivory Vinyl & Dark Green & White Herring-bone Weave
India Black	yes	—	yes	yes	yes	yes	—	yes
Superior Blue Met.	yes	—	—	yes	—	yes	—	—
Banff Blue	—	—	—	yes	—	yes	—	—
Glenwood Gray	yes	yes	yes	yes	yes	yes	—	yes
Beechwood Brn Met.	—	yes	yes	—	yes	—	yes	yes
Tahiti Tan	—	yes	yes	—	yes	—	yes	yes
Mohawk Maroon Met	yes	—	—	yes	—	yes	yes	—
Sherwood Green Met.	—	—	yes	—	yes	—	—	yes
Village Green Met.	—	yes	yes	—	yes	—	yes	yes
Pinehurst Green	—	yes	yes	—	yes	—	yes	yes

★ Monterey Coupe in above colors plus *Yosemite Yellow*, and *Bittersweet* with five distinct interior options

CONVERTIBLE AND STATION WAGON COLOR COMBINATIONS

Body Color	Red & Black Vinyl & Leather	Blue & Ivory Vinyl & Leather	Turq/Black & Ivory Vinyl & Leather	Yellow Black Vinyl & Leather	Bitter-sweet & Ivory Vinyl & Leather	Red, Tan, & Ivory Woven Plastic	Turq., Tan, & Ivory Woven Plastic
India Black	yes	—	yes	yes	yes	yes	yes
Superior Blue Met.	—	yes	—	—	—	—	yes
Banff Blue	—	yes	—	—	—	yes	—
Glenwood Gray	yes	yes	yes	yes	—	yes	—
Beechwood Brown Met.	—	—	yes	—	—	yes	yes
Tahiti Tan	yes	yes	yes	—	yes	yes	yes
Mohawk Maroon Met.	yes	—	—	—	—	yes	—
Sherwood Green Met.	—	—	yes	—	—	—	yes
Village Green Met.	—	—	yes	—	—	—	yes
Pinehurst Green	—	—	yes	—	yes	—	yes
Yosemite Yellow	—	yes	—	yes	—	—	—
Bittersweet	—	—	—	—	yes	—	—
Siren Red	yes	—	—	—	—	—	—

Convertible top material is *Black* with *Black* binding, *Black* with *Red* binding, *Gray-Tan* with matching binding, and *Green* with matching binding.

CLOSED CAR TWO-TONE COLOR COMBINATIONS

UPPER	LOWER	UPPER	LOWER
India Black	*Pinehurst Green*	*Banff Blue*	*Superior Blue Metallic*
India Black	*Village Green Metallic*	*Glenwood Gray*	*Superior Blue Metallic*
India Black	*Tahiti Tan*	*India Black*	*Glenwood Gray*
India Black	*Mohawk Maroon Metallic*	*Sherwood Green Metallic*	*Pinehurst Green*
India Black	*Banff Blue*	*Village Green Metallic*	*Pinehurst Green*
India Black	*Yosemite Yellow*	*Tahiti Tan*	*Mohawk Maroon Metallic*
India Black	*Bittersweet*	*Tahiti Tan*	*Beechwood Brown Metallic*
Tahiti Tan	*Bittersweet*		

Thirteen color combinations of vinyls, leathers, and woven cloths to harmonize

The official Pace Car and its escort in the pits at the 1953 Indianapolis "500" race.

As classy in their time as the 1932 Fords were in theirs, the 1953 Ford and Mercury cars would be the last of the famous "flathead V8's". It would be fitting that the cars bowed out on the 50th anniversary of the Ford Motor Company's founding, and that a gold, red, and blue commemorative medallion was placed on the top of the steering column of each 1953 Ford car to mark the event. In the following year the era of the overhead-valve Ford V8 would begin.

Flagship of the 1953 Ford line was the striking Pace Car Convertible that was exquisitely finished in Sungate Ivory with gold trim and special wire wheels. The famous car was also fitted with Coronado deck spare, dual spot lights, rocker panel trim, and rear bumper shields. It is now on exhibit at the Henry Ford Museum in Dearborn.

1952-53 GENUINE FORD AND MERCURY ACCESSORIES

OPTIONAL (or standard) ON ALL CARS

Radio, Heater, Defroster, Seat Covers, Road Lamps, WSW Tires, Spot Light, Sideview Mirror, Cigar Lighter, Locking Gas Cap, License Frames, Governor, Underseal, Back-up Lights, Windshield Washers, Non-Glare Mirror, Hand Brake Signal, Rear Window Defroster, Auto. Rear Door Locks, Exhaust Deflector, Grille Guard, Rocker Panel Trim, Spot Light with Mirror, Port. Utility Light, Windshield Visor, Rear Seat Speakers, Courtesy Lamp, Wheel Trim Rings, Custom Steering Wheel, Fender Shields, Full Hubcaps.

FORD OPTIONS

Turn Indicators	*Door-top Side Mirror*	*Door-belt Side Mirror*
Clamp-on Side Mirror	*Signal Viewer*	*Bumper Guards*
☆ *Rear Deck Guard*	*Floor Mats*	*Electric Clock*
Stem Wind Clock	*Glove Comp. Light*	*Window Vent Shades*
Coronado Deck Kit	*Hood Ornament*	

☆ 1952 item

MERCURY OPTIONS

Rear Window Wiper	★ *Door Edge Guard*	★ *Door Handle Shield*
Cowl Scuff Panels	*Gas Lid Lock*	*Curb Signal*
Vent Window Deflector	★ *Sea-tint Windows*	★ *Headlamp Door*
Underhood Insulation		

★ 1952 item

This list was taken directly from the Accessory Section of the Ford Body Parts Catalog. Parts easily interchanged between years but stars indicate model year the part was originally designated for. Many of the Ford items came standard on the Mercury.

PICTURE CREDITS

7: Gary Perrin, 8-12: Ford Archives, 13-14: Clarence Bullwinkle, 15: (top) University of Louisville, (bottom) Bob Lichty, 16-17: Dick Whittington, 18-22: Ford Archives, 23: (top) Indianapolis Speedway, 24-27: Ford Archives, 28-29: University of Louisville, 31: John A. Conde, 32-33: University of Louisville, 34-35: (top) Ford Archives, (bottom) University of Louisville, 36: (top) Ford Archives, (bottom) John A. Conde, 37: Indianapolis Speedway, 38-44: Ford Archives, 45: (top) Ford Archives, (bottom) University of Louisville, 46: (top two) Ford Archives, (bottom) University of Louisville, 47: University of Louisville, 48: Ford Archives, 49: (top photos) Ford Archives, (bottom photo) University of Louisville, 51: (top) Ford Archives, (bottom) University of Louisville, 52: Ford Archives, 53: University of Louisville, 54: (top) Dick Whittington, (bottom) Ford Archives, 55: (top) University of Louisville, (bottom two) Ford Archives, 56 (top) Ford Archives, (bottom) University of Louisville, 57: (top) Ford Archives, (bottom) Indianapolis Speedway, 58-61: Ford Archives, 62: John A. Conde, 63: Ford Archives, 64-67: John A. Conde, 68-70: Ford Archives, 70-71: (across bottom) University of Louisville, 72-75: University of Louisville, 76: John A. Conde, 77: Ford Archives, 78-79: Dick Whittington, 80: Ford Archives, 81: (top) Ford Archives, (bottom) University of Louisville, 82-83: University of Louisville, 84: Ford Archives, 85: (top) University of Louisville, (bottom) Ford Archives, 86: University of Louisville, 87-95: Ford Archives, 97-101: University of Louisville, 102-108: Ford Archives, 109: (top) Ford Archives, (bottom) University of Louisville, 110-111: Ford Archives, 112: University of Louisville, 113: Ford Archives, 114: University of Louisville, 115: Ford Archives, 116: (top three) Ford Archives, (bottom) University of Louisville, 117: (top) University of Louisville, (bottom) Ford Photomedia, 118: (top and bottom left) Ford Archives, (top and bottom right) University of Louisville, 119-125: Ford Photomedia, 126-127: Ford Archives, 128-133: Ford Photomedia, 134: Ford Archives, 135-137: Ford Photomedia, 138 (top) Ford Archives, (bottom) University of Louisville, 139-140: Ford Archives, 142: University of Louisville, 143: Ford Archives, 144: University of Louisville, 145-147: Ford Archives, 148-149: University of Louisville, 151: Dick Whittington, 152-157: Ford Archives, 158: University of Louisville, 159-165: Ford Archives, 167: Ford Photomedia, 168-169: University of Louisville, 170-184: Ford Photomedia, 186: University of Louisville, 187-239: Ford Photomedia.

BIBLIOGRAPHY

Company Literature:

Ford Assembly Change Letters, Ford Service Letters, Ford General Sales Letters, Ford and Mercury Body Parts Lists, Ford and Mercury Chassis Parts Catalogs, Ford and Mercury Passenger Car Sales Handbooks, 1946-53 Automotive Assembly Division production records, Ford and Mercury Sales Literature.

Books and Periodicals:

Ford News, Automotive Industries, The V8 Times, Ford: Decline and Rebirth.

THE AUTHOR

Lorin Sorensen has been researching and writing Ford Motor Company history for nearly two decades.

From 1967 to 1971 he was editor of *The V8 Times*, official publication of the Early Ford V8 Club of America; from 1970 to 1974 he edited and published *Ford Life* magazine; from 1973 to 1976 he edited and published *The Restorer*, the official publication of the Model A Ford Club of America; in 1978 he authored *The Ford Road* commemorating the 75th Anniversary of Ford Motor Company. From 1975 to the present he has also authored four volumes of a planned six book series about Ford automotive history.